Adult Non-Fiction

Inspirational

OVERCOMER
By God's Grace

A Memoir

Joi' Jno-Baptiste

This is a Non-fictional book. The events are factual by my own account. Some names and identifying details of people described in this book have been altered to protect their privacy.

Editing and Consulting by: Ready Writer Services, LLC

First Edition printed: April 2020

Printed in the United States of America

ISBN: 978-0-578-77883-9

Published by

Joi' Jno-Baptiste

PO Box 5403

Delanco, New Jersey 08075

Author's Contact Information:

Website: www.joijno-baptiste.com

Email: joi@joijno-baptiste.com

Acknowledgments

On September 6, 2019, I was commissioned by God to write the pages of my life while attending the Prophetic Encounter Service. It is my prayer that each page of my life's journey encourages, uplifts, motivates, and warns each person who reads this book. It is also my prayer that you draw near to God and stay close to Him as you go through your journey of this life. For it is only Him that will Keep YOU, Guide YOU, Love YOU, Comfort YOU, Protect YOU, Heal YOU, Pick YOU Up and Turn YOU Around and Make YOU, too, an Overcomer by God's Grace.

I Thank God for Jesus, I Thank God for Courage, I Thank God for Strength, I Thank God for Peace and His Joy, I Thank God for Freedom, and I Thank God for generational curses broken off my life, off my children's lives, off my family's lives, and off your life, for we are all Victorious People.

"And we know that all things work together for good to them that love God, to them who are the called according to his purpose." Romans 8:28

In Dedication

Dad and Mom

Sharell, Brandy and Davon

I Love You All Always and Forever

TABLE OF CONTENTS

HOPE

*"Therefore I will look unto the Lord; I will wait for
the God of my salvation: my God will hear me."*
Micah 7:7

---⟨◊⟩---

nother Friday night, my father could not wait to hit
the club scene. "Just got paid, Friday night party
hunting," was the song my mother and my sisters;
Sharell, Brandy, and I heard blasting upstairs as my father
showered and dressed in his finest party clothing. The smell
of cologne filled the air as we sat downstairs watching
another episode of the Golden Girls. Sharell was two years
older than me, and Brandy was five years younger than me.
They seemed not to care about our father going out to party.
I would always try to block out the fact that my father was
leaving us, for I knew it would be morning before I would
see him again. I tried to prolong him from leaving, I would
think of the oddest things a nine-year-old could talk about. I
remember one time having a conversation with my father
that went like, "Hey dad, do you know the names of the
planets in the solar system?" He appeared to be listening, but
then he replied, "Umm hum, ay Joi' pass me my black socks
over there on top of the dresser," as he greased and brushed
his hair. My conversation was the furthest thing on his mind.
My father had worked all week, and he had a one-track

mind. He wanted to dance to the beat of the grooving sounds of some of the eighty's R&B singers and groups like Morris Day and the Time, Billy Ocean, and Freddie Jackson, while making jokes with his friends. My father's weekly responses often left me feeling alone with a void inside. I would often go to my room, having conversations with myself. I remember saying, "Does he not love me more than going to a club to party or hanging out with his friends drinking and dancing the night away?" It seemed as though Friday and some Saturday nights of partying had become my father's weekly tradition. This was a feeling I was tired of, so I vowed to myself to never be like my father when I had children. My father seldom did much with Sharell, Brandy, or myself; no bedtime stories, no helping with homework, and no real affection. He never invested time with us to build healthy relationships. My father and mother seemed to barely agree on anything or show us any real family structure. I often thought and even said out loud when angry, "I can't wait to grow up," for I wanted a better life for myself. I had hoped, as a little girl, that God would allow my father to stay home with my mother, Sharell, Brandy, and me so we could be a happy family. The kind of family I often saw on television, like on the Cosby Show, 227, and Good Times. They always seemed loving and caring towards each other.

Once my father was ready to showcase his attire before leaving, he would come downstairs looking like a backup old school blues singer. All he needed was a microphone. He wore his weekly gold and black striped shirt half-buttoned showing a small portion of his bare chest. His super pressed gold pants looked like a shiny gold candy wrapper with his freshly glistened black dress shoes he had just shined upstairs in the bathroom. He would say, "Alright y'all, I'm out." Sharell, Brandy, and I would just give him a wave while my mother would just give him a displeased look. My mother was not into going to clubs to party, but I knew if my father had asked her to party with him, she would have found a babysitter for my sisters and me quickly. As night fell, my mother, my sisters, and I watched Karate Kid and E.T. while eating snacks snuggled under our blankets. We watched the same two movies almost every weekend. It seemed as if we knew every word to the movie and when to laugh. We made the best of our evening by spending time together. I enjoyed this time, I just wished my father were home to join us. Soon one by one, we all marched to our beds, calling it a night.

Bang...Bang...Bang was the sound I heard, early Saturday morning at our front door, "Open the door," my father shouted with a raspy voice. My father's voice and his banging on the door was the cause of my angry awakening. Brandy attempted to open the door. However, Sharell and I knew not to go near the door to open it. We did not want to feel my mother's wrath. She would yell, "Get away from the door," with fire coming out of her mouth. A fire that would burn Sharell and I if we opened the door, so we knew to always stand clear of the door when my father began banging. My mother was fully dressed, with a scarf on her head. I could hear her saying as she walked down the steps, "He stayed out all night, now he come bring his ass in here at 9:30 in the damn morning." My father had a key to the door; however, he seemed never to be able to open the door. Perhaps, he was too drunk to figure out which key was the correct key. Whatever the reason for my father's inability to open the door, my mother would make him wait until she was ready to let him inside. "Open the door," my father would plead and plead again, maybe ten times before my mother would open the door.

Once she opened the door, the sound of profanity became their fluent first language they spoke to each other almost every Saturday morning. Then the fighting began with sometimes my father pushing or hitting my mother as he staggered up the steps to get in their bed so that he could sleep. A scene he had often witnessed, as a child, from his father who also partied on the weekends. However, my Grandfather would leave on Friday and not return until Sunday. As my father slept his morning away, my mother sat on the couch, with the facial expression of a pit bull. The look of her disgruntled face made me and my sisters cautious not to get in her way. We knew not to ask her for anything or not even to quarrel amongst ourselves. We knew we would feel her hand on our backside if we did.

Although my father's morning arrival angered my mother, she was right by his side when he would have a seizure in bed while sleeping. It was like her ears had two antennas, listening for the sound of thumping, as my father would fall out of the bed, often hitting his head against the floor. My mother would go right into action. Rushing up the stairs two steps at a time, to hold my father's body tight, manhandling him to place him on his side as his body jerked uncontrollably. My mother would make Sharell, Brandy, and me go back downstairs, telling us to close their bedroom door as we tried to get a glimpse of my father. My father would often forget to take his medication for his seizure disorder. A disorder he received at the age of eighteen after he was hit by a car while riding his bike. He was in a coma for more than two months. His sister, Aunt Beth once told me when he came out of the coma, he was never the same. She described how my father's mood had changed from pleasant, helpful, and full of life to angry, selfish, and withdrawn at times.

When my father had awakened from his long morning slumber, he would seem as if nothing ever happened. My sisters and I did too. My mother, on the other hand, had little to nothing to say to him. It would be another weekend of doing the same thing. My mother never really wanted to do anything. She always said she did not have any money.

"With what?" were her two favorite words she used to answer my questions when I would ask her about going somewhere fun. I would often ask, "Ma, can we go to the movies?" Her response would be, "With what?" I would later ask, "Ma, can we go to the park?" Again, her response would be, "With what?" It appeared she became comfortable answering me with her two favorite words every weekend.

My mother worked as a cafeteria worker at the local elementary school in the mornings and as a custodial worker cleaning office buildings in the evenings, five days a week. My father worked five days a week as a parks and recreation attendant. My mother made sure my sisters and I had food, clothes, shoes; and she made sure to keep our hair combed and neat. As a child, I knew my mother's responsibilities for my sisters and me were great. I sometimes understood why her answer to my questions was "With what?" It was possible she did not have much money left. Not so much for my father, he maintained the rent and utilities nothing more. My sisters and I knew not to ask him for anything, he never seemed to want to be bothered.

Sharell and I tried to make the best of our weekends by doing things like hanging outside with the neighborhood kids. Meanwhile, Brandy stayed in the house with my mother and father. Sharell and I hated to take her with us outside because we would have to watch her. My mother always told Sharell and I to stay together and not to go inside our friend's house. Although we agreed, we never listened.

As soon as we went outside, we went in separate directions to our friends' houses. Sharell and I did not have the same friends, Sharell hung out with the older girls, while I played with the kids that were my age. Once we knocked on their door and they opened it, we went inside to play or to hangout.

I always went to my friend Nya's house to play with her baby dolls or to play Mario and Duck Hunt on her Nintendo while eating her snacks. Nya was an only child. She had more dolls and snacks than the toy and grocery stores. My parents seldom purchased snacks for us, and when they did in a day or two days, the snacks would be gone. I was always in heaven when I was at Nya's house. It was my escape from all the yelling, cursing, and fighting I would often see between my parents. Nya and I would challenge each other to see who could play Mario or Duck Hunt the longest before losing, and we both hated to lose.

One time while at Nya's house, I lost track of time trying to win a game of Duck Hunt. I heard my mother calling my name near Nya's house. I could hear the anger in her voice as she yelled my name. It was like each syllable of my name had a fireball attached to it. My heart gripped with fear. Nya and I looked at each other as if my mother knew I was in her house. I dropped the remote controller and yelled to Nya, "See you on Monday at school," as I leaped down her steps before unlocking and running out her back door. I was too afraid my mother would see me leaving out of her front door.

Once outside, I ran all the way home, which was just two housing sections away. I was a self-made track star that day. I was hoping my mother did not see me as I sprinted home. My goal was to beat her back home, which I did.

I ran straight to my room, skipping the ten, now five, steps. I saw Sharell watching TV, I thought, *'Dang, how did she beat me home?'* Sharell always knew how never to get caught. I took off my coat and started playing with my radio, trying to find a slow song to calm my racing heart and mind because I knew I was caught. New Edition's "If It Isn't Love" was all I could find on my one speaker radio. I loved Ralph, I often thought, when I finished high school, he would find me and take me away to a big house with bright colors and a swimming pool in the backyard.

As I sang along to Ralph's part, I heard my mother come into the house. She yelled upstairs, "Joi', where you been? Come down here." This was really when I hoped Ralph popped out of the radio to take me away, forget waiting for high school. Once downstairs I knew not to lie to my mother, but to save myself from a whooping, I replied "Ma, I was upstairs playing with my dolls, I thought I heard you outside calling my name, but I just waited for you to come back in the house to see what you wanted." Then the look of that pit bull came across her face, that same pit bull look I saw early this morning when my father arrived home. I knew she knew I was lying. She said, "Oh you lying now?" and before I knew it I felt one hand hit my back and then the other hand hit my leg, she gave me several smacks before sending me upstairs to my room. "And clean them clothes off the floor in your closet," she yelled as I walked up the steps crying.

From that day forward, I made sure to be in front of my house before the streetlight came on and not to stay too long in Nya's house. Enough time to play one game and to get a few snacks before leaving. My mother was extremely strict, she had no time for foolishness. She made sure we followed her rules and completed our chores. My parents were not hard on Sharell and me about our academics until we received a bad grade. Then they would yell at us, followed by a whooping as if they offered to help us complete an assignment or study for a spelling or math test. Sharell once told her school's Guidance Counselor that my mother whooped her because of her unacceptable grades on her report card. The Guidance Counselor called my mother to discuss the matter and proceeded to send a Child Protective Services worker to our house to walk through our home and to talk to my mother and Sharell. Once the woman left, my mother gave Sharell another whooping. I was shocked and scared, and I thought Sharell was going into foster care. She had broken my mother's Golden Rule, which was, whatever happened in our house, stayed in our house. Sharell and I made sure to never let our friends or anybody know about the dysfunction that was going on in our home or the fact that our parents were using drugs.

My father was a fan of marijuana, almost every Saturday while listening to Cameo's "Word Up." My father would lay on the living room floor dressed in a tight faded blue t-shirt and blue basketball shorts that he may have worn in high school with white socks that came up to his knees. He would use his favorite rap group, Whodini's album cover, to break up his marijuana. He would then peel off one white tissue paper to fill it up with marijuana, before rolling it up tightly and licking the tissue paper as if it were an envelope, he was ready to seal. Lastly, he would light his neatly perfected joint to smoke it. The long-lasting aroma would soon fill the air in our compact living room as my father laid in the middle of the floor, smoking. My father was incredibly open with his marijuana use. He did not care if the President of the United States came over, he would have no thought of breaking out his weed to break up, roll up, and smoke. He might have even offered the President one.

My mother, on the other hand, was very private with her cocaine use. She would always make sure she gave Sharell, Brandy, and me something to do, or she would have given us a snack, so we would never interrupt her or notice she had gone into the bathroom. She would go into the bathroom and take a blast, often leaving the angle cut clear straw piece in the bathroom on the floor with residue left behind in the straw. Sharell and I knew what had gone down after my mother came out of the bathroom. We gave each other the eye knowing my mother had gotten high. Even though we were kids, we knew more than what our parents thought. We also knew not to say anything about what we knew, not even to each other. I was sure my father was aware, however, I never heard him mention my mother's drug use to her or her friends.

Sharell and I were close. We always tried to block out the dysfunction in our home by creating rap songs or daring each other to do things that we knew we should not do. Like the time Sharell dared me to steal forty dollars from her friend, Mia, in our neighborhood who had been bragging about having the money. And, like a professional thief, I did it. We laughed all the way home as we split the money before creating a good story to tell our parents. We knew they would know we had money, by the way we were acting. However, when Sharell and I would disagree and continue with an argument, her true feelings about me were revealed. She would always call me a white girl and laugh at how light my skin complexion was, while making fun of my skinny legs or how crooked my teeth were. Sharell and Brandy's skin complexion was much browner than mine. Sharell would never let me forget how she felt about me once she was mad at me. I would make jokes about how often she stuttered when trying to finish her sentences and how she could not fight. Although she could fight, I just wanted her to feel how she made me feel, sad. Without showing it to Sharell, her words always penetrated deep into my mind, sometimes making me dislike who I was. Playing make-believe and playing with baby dolls with Brandy always took my mind off what was going on in our home and the words Sharell and I spoke to each other. Now knowing, it was a ripple effect of the spirit that was operating in our house.

Although my father partied on Friday nights and some Saturday nights, he would get up faithfully to go to church every Sunday. First thing Sunday morning, he was awake playing the Commodores. He would loudly sing along to his favorite *"Sunday get ready for church"* song. He would sing, "That's why I'm easy, I'm easy like Sunday morning" as he coughed to clear his throat after missing one or two notes. He would then play, "Jesus Is Love," while standing in the mirror singing the whole song before gathering me and my sisters in the car. We would pack into my father's '83 Chevrolet Chevette and head off to church. My father always made sure we were on time for church, and, if we were running late, he would make a big fuss, often making me feel like I just wanted to stay home. While at church, I would just sit and watch my father as he sang in the choir during Sunday service. I would wonder how my father could party on the weekend, repeatedly smoke marijuana, fight with his wife, spend no time with his children yet attend church faithfully, and sing as if the words he was singing were the life he was living. I looked over at Mrs. Mary as she handed me and my sisters a piece of peppermint candy. I thanked her with a smile before staring back at my father.

Every Sunday, Mrs. Mary would give me and my sisters peppermint candy. This was sometimes the happiest part of attending church. My mother just sat looking pleasant, seemingly absorbing the Word from the sermon preached by Reverend Moses. It was as if the message was giving her the strength to get through the week to come.

It was difficult being in fourth grade and coming back to school every week from a dysfunctional weekend. My classmates often asked, "Joi', what did you do this weekend?" as they could not wait to discuss their exciting weekend. I would rehearse what I was going to say in the mirror before I arrived at school Monday. I wanted to make sure my lies made sense and had plenty of substance. I always made sure I included my family in whatever I lied about doing. "Well, my family and I went to the movies to see Beetlejuice after school on Friday. Then my sisters and I went to my cousin's slumber party on Saturday. On Sunday, I went to church with my family." These were events I wanted to do with my family. However, all I could think about was my mother's two favorite words, "With what?" whenever I was asked about what I did over the weekend. I wanted to fit in with my peers, who always seemed to attend some type of fun-filled events with their family.

Having a lot of friends and fitting in were my two main goals. However, I never seemed to be able to obtain the two. I was the tall, super thin girl with medium length hair and crooked teeth from sucking my thumb, a thumb I often found comfort in. I felt like I stuck out due to my weight and height. I was not sure if these features were a sign of weakness or frailness to others. However, despite my physical appearance, I sometimes felt I was different from my peers. I would often talk about God and how He has a plan for His people. Though I meant good by what I believed, I was not always accepted by my peers. Some would find any reason to dislike me, some of the girls would say, "You think you cute, or why you be wearing your hair like that?" or "Girl, your legs are boney." Often wanting to fight me when I challenged them. I remember five girls in the fourth grade at my elementary school who did not like me, and I never knew why. Every morning, I would see them standing in the hall near my class. One of the taller girls in the group would say, "There she goes, look at her." They would roll their eyes at me and laugh loudly as if they wanted everyone to hear them. I never responded to any of them, I went to my class as expected. I was not sure if my lack of response made them mad, but if they were looking for a reaction, I never gave one.

One day when walking to my bus, the five girls tried to jump me. I saw them running after me, the tallest one saying, "There she goes, get her." I began running to my bus, trying not to fall as I ran through other students walking to their bus. I had never run so fast on my bus before. All I thought of was getting on the bus, and that's what I did. I always hated when their bus number and my bus number was called at the same time. I knew they would be waiting for me. I often prayed, "Lord, please don't let them big girls' bus number be called at the same time as mine." I even told Sharell, so we both could confront them, but she seemed to never be around. I hated going to school, I remember having thoughts that if I had Salt-N-Pepa around, they could protect me. They were the biggest girl rap group out at the time, and they appeared tough. I knew those girls would never try to bully or fight me again. They would try to be my friend, which was what I wanted. It was all wishful thinking.

At lunch, I sat with my classmates. I would see the five of them mean-mugging and rolling their eyes at me when they entered the cafeteria. Though my heart would start racing after seeing the first girl enter, I would just look the other way or act as though I did not see them. I never understood why someone who has never had a conversation or played with me at the school's playground could just hate me as much as these girls did. Until one day, I went to a Girl Scouts meeting with my neighborhood friend, Mya, and I saw three of the girls who did not like me. They never said much to me. They just stared at me as if they had forgotten how they were running after me three weeks ago when I was walking to my bus. I too, acted as if I did not know the girls during the Girl Scouts meeting. The next day at school, when the five of them saw me, they just acted like they did not see me. The tallest girl, the ringleader had nothing to say, she just stared at me, wanting to say something, but God would not allow her. I thought, "Thank you Lord," they have finally left me alone.

I was so glad when the school year ended. My mother, my sisters, and I took the five-hour journey to my Grandma's house in New Jersey for the summer. I loved going to Grandma's house in the summer. There were no fights, no arguments to hear, and it was always a fun time with my cousins. I also had one on one time with Grandma, which made my summer at her house all more worthwhile. The night before leaving for New Jersey, my mother made fried chicken sandwiches and packed plenty of snacks. Because once we got on the road, there was no stopping unless we had to go to the restroom. As we left, one by one, we kissed my father goodbye as he seemed unbothered that we were leaving him for two months. My mother would say, "95 North here we come" as we rode in her brand new '88 Pontiac Sunbird. She could not wait to put her car on the road and show it off to Grandma.

My mother loved music. She blasted the tunes of Keith Sweat, Guy, Alexander O'Neal, Al B. Sure, and Karen White the whole ride to Grandma's house. We laughed, danced, and sung most of the five-hour trip. It was as if my mother was another fun-filled, excited person. A person simply happy she would be getting a break from my sisters and me for two months. I was glad to see her in such a good mood.

16

Once at Grandma's house, Sharell, Brandy, and I were greeted with a great big hug from Grandma. Her breasts were big enough to swallow us whole. She was a stout woman who stood at about 5'5. She had long gray hair, and she had hands that could tell a story of how hard she had worked throughout her forty-nine years of life. She said, "Look at you Joi', we got to fatten you up looking like your daddy tall and skinny" while she laughed at the size of my thin legs. Sharell and Brandy looked at me, filled with anguish. I just smiled as I was carefully examined by Grandma. My mother showed off her new car before leaving to drive back to Virginia. Grandma drove the car around the corner and back before drilling my mother with several financial questions. My mother sarcastically answered each one as I listened from a distance. I must admit, I was an inquisitive little girl. I wanted to know everything that was going on with my mother, who I sometimes worried about without telling her. I made sure every night to pray that God would cover her and protect her while my sisters and I were away from her.

My four cousins Tameka (age eight), Madalyn (age seven), Ronald (age six), and Ashley (age two), who lived with my Grandma, were so happy to see my sisters and me, and we were just as excited to see them. We would all wake up together, eat lunch together, fight with each other; but at the end of the day, we all loved and cared for each other. I often thought this is how a family should be. When it was time for bed, we would make pallets with our blankets on the floor of the living room, where we would sleep until morning. Once we all had awakened, we had cereal to eat for breakfast. Grandma also made homemade biscuits some mornings for the now seven of us. She would serve the biscuits with thick brown molasses. I hated the smell and the taste of the molasses, but she made sure I ate at least one biscuit before leaving the table. Grandma made sure we always had food to eat. Once she noticed there was little food, she would sit at the kitchen table, dig in her bra, and pull out a long black stocking. Grandma intensely unraveled the rubber bands off her money. Once she removed the thick stack of money from her stocking, she would give my eldest cousin some money and instruct him of the types of food to purchase from the grocery store.

Grandma allowed us to have the freedom to go places my parents did not take my sisters and me. Grandma allowed us to walk to the local shopping plaza and gave us each ten dollars to purchase whatever we wanted. We were also allowed to walk to the park, we loved to play on the swings and the tall slide. We even stayed outside when it was dark, as long as we were in front of her house. We could walk to different places if an older cousin came along with us. With that being said, it was a group of seven of us from the smallest to the biggest.

On Saturday mornings, Grandma would take me with her to clean her customers' houses. The houses were the size of houses seen in magazines. Some had tall ceilings with several sky views, kitchens with marble counters and plush carpet, the kind you would make your guests take their shoes off to walk on. I was incredibly careful to do just what Grandma directed me to do. I was glad she always asked me to clean with her on Saturdays. Going to clean with Grandma allowed me to have time alone with her. I enjoyed one on one time with Grandma, she mainly instilled in me the importance of keeping a clean house. Grandma did not play around with my cousins or me about cleaning her house either, she made sure we kept her house clean. If it was not clean, we were sure to get a smacking on our backside, no matter if we were asleep or awake. After we were done cleaning the customer's house, Grandma would give me twenty dollars for helping her. We would listen to the grooving sounds of Marvin Gaye and Tammy Terrell as she drove back home in her '85 Cadillac Fleetwood Brougham.

Every Saturday evening, my cousins and I would help Grandma place tables in her backyard to decorate with candles before placing the chairs under each table. Later at night, she would have her friends over for drinking, music, and dancing. Grandma would have so much alcohol. She never missed the few beers Sharell, Tameka, and I took while watching Grandma and her friends. We watched from upstairs in her bedroom window as her backyard filled up with her friends from church and others we had never seen. One by one, the tables became occupied with laughter while the sounds of smooth jazz and Motown singers created a sound that blasted throughout the backyard. Tameka and I laughed as Mrs. Linda and Mr. Charles danced to Marvin Gaye and Tammi Terrell's "Ain't, No Mountain High Enough." It would not be long before Grandma, and her friends would all begin dancing. The women were swaying their hips from side to side as their arms reached out to grab their partner's hands as they danced the night away to the well-known tunes. Grandma's backyard was full of her friends, creating a beautiful picture of laughter, loud conversation, and dancing. I could not wait to experience this happy feeling when I grew up. I imagined dancing the night away, even if I was the only one dancing and the music had stopped. I would dance away every feeling and negative emotion I had been carrying.

Grandma made sure we attended church while staying at her house for the summer. She would shop at the local thrift store and purchase clothes for us to wear to church on Sunday. She washed and ironed the clothes as she taught us the words to the song, we were to sing Sunday morning in the children's choir. "I'll Fly Away" was the name of one of the songs I remember. Though we were too young to understand the meaning of the song, we sang as instructed, making Grandma proud. Being around Grandma gave me Hope. I Hoped to know that, if I pray to God, He will help me get through anything. Grandma taught my cousins and me the Lord's prayer. She would pray at night and often read her Bible before going to bed. Though I did not say much, I watched her as if I was studying for a test. Grandma was my only real example of knowing the True and Living God, the God that raised Jesus from the cross, the God that created the universe. That God!

Once summer was over, my sisters and I headed back to Virginia. My parents moved our family into a new two-bedroom apartment. It was everything but bigger than our last apartment. The rooms reminded me of a small box. I could turn around and feel like I was in another room. It was that small. The streets were filled with loud talking and laughter from school-aged kids who were playing kickball and dancing to the latest music. I loved our new environment. There were plenty of kids Sharell and my age. Some of the tall cute boys played basketball while the school-aged girls made up cheers that I wanted to learn. My parents were getting along, which made me happy. My father stopped partying on the weekends and stayed home with my mother, my sisters, and myself. This was a prayer I earnestly Hoped and prayed for, and I was glad God had answered my prayers. However, my father seemed to be working more hours on the weekends. When he was not working on the weekend, he was watching sports, often yelling at the television, complaining about how the players were playing. My father would often ask my sisters and me to watch the game with him. He would share his sunflower seeds with us while trying to explain the rules of the game. Brandy and Sharell were not interested, they seemed only to like the sunflower seeds. However, I was glad my father was home with us and even though I was not interested either, I paid attention to every detail of the game, as my father explained. This was the time I enjoyed being with my father. It was a time I felt close to him. A time I felt he cared.

In the fall of 1989, Sharell, Brandy, and I started new schools, and I was excited to meet new friends. This was my last year in elementary school. I was full of confidence throughout my fifth-grade year. I was never bullied. I seemed to fit in with a few girls in my class. I enjoyed my fifth-grade year at school, and I met my best friend, Lia. I enjoyed being around her family. Her parents seemed to genuinely love each other. There was no yelling or arguing, and Lia's family attended church as a family. One Sunday morning I attended Lia's church with her family. Lia's church was quite different from the Baptist services I was used to. Every woman who attended the church had on black and white with a cloth on their head. The service was normal to me until I noticed one woman jump up to dance like she was in a chicken coop as the musicians played on the organ and the drums. Her arms were by her sides, and she was moving her feet super-fast. Then I saw another woman jump up the same way dancing in front of the church. I quietly laughed to myself without wanting anyone to see me. I looked over at Lia as she clapped her hands and stomped her right foot. When I arrived home from church, I could not wait to tell Sharell and Brandy the dancing I observed at Lia's church. I laughed hysterically as I did the chicken dance in the middle of the floor. My sisters laughed too and began dancing with me like the woman from church. Little did we know, the woman was praising God.

On the weekends I would stay at Lia's house, I always made sure to do my chores and what was expected of me, so there was no reason for my mother to tell me I could not go to Lia's house. Towards the end of my fifth-grade year, I noticed my family seemed different. My mother worked a lot, and though my father was home with my sisters and me, he was not home as much in the evening. My sisters and I were close, but we never talked about our concerns with our parents. Although our parents were in our home, my sisters and I had no real relationship with them. If we took a picture, you would think we were one big happy family because our clothes matched, and our smiles were big and bright. Honestly, we just existed together.

Once my fifth-grade graduation came near, I told my mother weeks ahead so that she would attend. She told me she was going to try to take off from work. My mother was still working two jobs. There was no need to ask my father because I knew that he would not attend, despite being home at the time of my graduation. The night of my graduation, neither of my parents attended. I went to my graduation with Lia's family. After graduation, her mother took me back home. I was sad and disappointed because my mother did not attend my graduation. I received no flowers, no card, nor any gifts; it was as if nothing ever happened.

I wanted to go back to Grandma's house. I often called her to see how she was doing. Despite not being able to go back to Grandma's house, I continued to hold on to Hope in God that my life would become better. I continued to pray and had Hope, God would answer my prayers. "Therefore I will look unto the Lord; I will wait for the God of my salvation: my God will hear me."

COURAGE

"Have not I commanded thee? Be strong and of a good courage; be not afraid, neither be thou dismayed: for the LORD thy God is with thee whithersoever thou goest."
Joshua 1:9

———————◊———————

Duringmysecond year of middle school, my father began appearing more distant at times. We did not do anything as a family, there were no family night dinners out, no family trips to the amusement parks, no park visits, no family fun time, and we had stopped going to church. My father did not like a lot of noise, so he would become quickly agitated and would begin yelling at Sharell, Brandy, or me when one of us got in his way or did something he did not like. My mother and father's relationship was not appealing. My father would often yell and use profanity towards my mother in front of my sisters and me. It would not be long before my mother started going to nightclubs for drinking, and dancing. Sharell had the duty of watching Brandy and me. Although my father would be home, it was as though he was not there. He would stay in his room watching television and mainly come out of his room to eat or to use the restroom. While my mother was out looking to get her groove back, so was Sharell, who started having sex with one of the older boys in the neighborhood.

One Sunday afternoon, my mother took Sharell, Brandy, and me to the park where she met with a man she called her friend. He stood at about 6'3, around one hundred and seventy-five pounds with a dark skin tone. My mother introduced us to her friend and, one by one, we replied, "Hi" while wondering *'who is this man?'* I thought it was strange for my mother to introduce us to a man she called her friend. He had brought his three young children to the park as well. They all looked as though they just started walking. My sisters and I embraced them and played with them while at the park. At times, I watched my mother's interaction with her so-called friend while I was pretending to be playing. They appeared incredibly happy around each other, I had not seen my mother laugh and smile so much. On the ride back home, I asked the question my sisters wanted to ask but were too afraid to ask. With no regard for fear, I asked, "Mom, who was that man?" My mother quickly smiled and said, "He is just a friend that is all." In my clever mind, I knew she had some feelings for her so-called "friend."

Four months later, my parents separated. My mother asked my father to leave our apartment after finding drugs in their bedroom. I heard my parents arguing the day my mother asked my father to leave. She complained that my father's drug use was the reason he was not providing necessities for our family. Although my father was using drugs, my mother continued her drug use at a slower pace, which allowed her to continue to provide for my sisters and me. I started to believe this was the cause of my father's distant behavior, rapid mood swings, and agitation with us. I cannot say I was sad when my father left. It was like a spirit of heaviness had been lifted. Though it would be different without my father being in our home, I was excited about the change. Two weeks after my father left our apartment, Sharell told my mother she was pregnant. It was not be long before my mother took Sharell to have an abortion at the local clinic. However, once the procedure began, the doctor felt the baby's foot and told my mother and Sharell he would not be able to complete the procedure. My mother was enduring a lot of obstacles. My father had left, my sister was pregnant, and now my mother received a call from her employer informing her that her custodial position had been terminated.

My mother was home now in the evenings, which allowed her relationship with Sharell, Brandy, and me to become closer. Although my mother was home with us, we soon started to feel the financial loss take effect. We sometimes had very little food to eat. One time, we could only use the microwave to cook our food due to our gas utilities being disconnected. My mother frequently discussed her concerns about my father not making any financial contributions to our household, which soon led to my mother going to court to apply for child support. My mother was honest with my sisters and me about her financial hardships. We did not have to wonder why Christmas missed us or why we did not receive new clothes or shoes. My mother made it very clear she did not have any money to purchase most of our necessities. It was hard for her, most of the time she had no money to wash our clothes, put gas in her car, or pay her monthly bills. Though we struggled, we still had a close bond between the four of us. My sisters and I did our best not to put any further strains on our mother. When we wanted or needed anything, most of the time, we went without. I often prayed God would help my mother with her finances, for I hated seeing the stress on her face.

Within six months of my father leaving, one evening we received a knock on the door. When my mother opened the door, her face lit up like a Christmas tree. It was her so-called "friend" from the park. My mother had invited him to our house to formally introduce him to my sisters and me. Still glowing, she stood by the front door once he entered and said, "Sharell, Joi', and Brandy, this is Lehigh, y'all say hi." We all said, "Hi" in unison, like in a choir. This would be an introduction to many more visits from Lehigh. One day as usual, Lehigh had arrived at our house. Once he entered the living room, I quickly opened the closet door and told him to go inside, because my father was coming. When he went inside the closet, I shut the closet door. My sisters and I laughed so hard before I quickly opened the door. I heard my mother walking up the steps in our apartment building to come into the house. She would have given me several smacks if she knew what I had done. I did not like Lehigh, I did not like my mother throwing someone new on me and my sisters knowing my father had recently left. I started complaining about Lehigh to Sharell and Brandy, but they did not seem to care because they liked him. It was less than one year since my father had left, and my mother had begun dating someone new. This was difficult for me to digest. I was surprised my mother would bring another man into our house so fast. He began sleeping in the same bed my father used to sleep in, and he was now coming into our space as if he was filling in my father's place.

I started taking my frustrations out at school. I was rude and disrespectful to my math teacher, Mr. Fox. He was very patient with me, it was like he knew something was going on at home. He gave me several warnings and one in-school suspension. However, I still did not adhere to his warnings. One evening my mother told me she received a phone call from Mr. Fox. I knew I was about to get a whooping that would make me apologize and become respectful overnight. She talked to me about their phone conversation. Before she could finish, she broke out that brown leather belt from behind her back and gave me an old school behind whooping. I was so angry. I felt like nobody understood how I felt, and I was too afraid to tell my mother. It was like I had no outlet. I had not spoken to my father since he had left our apartment. Besides, it wasn't like he would do anything anyway.

In the Fall of 1991, Sharell delivered a healthy full-term baby boy named Michael. Once cleared to return to school by her doctor, she started her sophomore year of high school. My mother paid the neighbor Ms. Nancy weekly to care for Michael while Sharell attended school. This was an expense she would soon be unable to continue to pay. Despite Lehigh, who was now living with us, my mother's financial struggles continued. My mother called Grandma to share her concerns about not being able to care for both Sharell and her son, Michael. With no hesitation Grandma gave her approval of Sharell and Michael to live with her in New Jersey. The thought of Sharell and Michael leaving made me very sad and lonely. First, it was my father who left, and though I did not care at first, it was now bothering me. The day Sharell and Michael left to move to New Jersey, my heart felt heavy. I couldn't tell Sharell because I did not want her to cry. Brandy and I just hugged her and Michael before saying good-bye.

Once Sharell and Michael left, I would often see my mother and Lehigh share affection towards each other. I felt like my mother was now more into Lehigh than Brandy and me. I wanted to just talk to her to tell her my feelings, but it seemed to never be the right time, I was also just scared of her reaction. I often prayed, asking God to help Brandy and me and, most of all, to help my mother, who had begun using drugs again. I was not sure if Brandy knew, and I refused to discuss it with her. I just tried to stay strong for her and sometimes I made her laugh to keep my mind off my problems at home. Within one year of Sharell and Michael going to New Jersey, my mother was no longer able to maintain her bills. We were evicted from our apartment. My mother's car was repossessed, and my mother and Lehigh had ended their relationship. My mother called Grandma to ask her if we could live with her until she could regain stability. Grandma agreed. Within one week, my mother, Brandy, and I boarded a Greyhound bus and headed to New Jersey. I was so glad to see Grandma, my cousins, Sharell, and most of all, Michael. It was the best reunion.

My mother soon enrolled Brandy and me into school. Often, I would walk home with one of my friends, Sonya. Sonya and I used to hang out when I would come to Grandma's house for the summer. Sonya was cool, she was from North Philadelphia. She knew the ins and outs of things in the area, she was way more street advanced than me. Sonya would tell me how to stay to myself and not befriend a lot of people at school. She put me on to not letting my classmates know where I lived, since I was new to the school. You see, it was like a housing section gang. If you lived in a certain part of the small suburb and that section did not like the other sections, there would be some verbal or physical exchange. I once saw a group of boys fight another group of boys just because the two sections where the boys lived did not like each other. I was not afraid, but I felt as if I had entered a war zone. I wondered, "Where did my mother move us to?" I was from the inner city, where I saw action at school, but I had never been exposed to this type of school environment.

On the weekends, I would go to my Aunt Linda's house to hang out with my cousin Tameka and her friends. I couldn't wait for the weekend. There was always something fun to do. We would hang out at the pizza shops at night or go to house parties near Tameka's house. We hung out with some of the boys from her neighborhood. I used to like Jose, who hung out with us. I would often sing Mary J. Blige's "You Remind Me" or "Real Love" when I would see him. I sang in my head because if he heard me singing, he might have walked away. I tried to be like cousin Tameka and her friends. I soon started smoking cigarettes, Black & Mild cigars, and drinking beer. I always wanted Jose to see me doing these things. I wanted to be cool like everyone else and stand out at the same time. At times, I would also talk about God and how we needed to live right so we could be used by Him. However, none of the girls were interested, they would often just laugh at me and tell me how crazy I sounded talking about God after I had just drunk a cup of Olde English 800.

Although Aunt Linda was home, sometimes it was as if she was not there. We had little supervision and we were able to be our free-hearted selves. One day while walking to the store, I was smoking a Kool cigarette while talking to Tameka and her friends Shay, Rhonda, and Kim. Suddenly, I swallowed the smoke while talking. The smoke was so thick my chest started hurting, and then my heart started beating super fast. I felt like I was in panic mode. I felt like I had lost my breath, I just stood still coughing and watching Tameka and her friends laugh hysterically. I gestured to Tameka that I had swallowed the cigarette smoke as I coughed. I was so scared, all I could do was try to catch my breath. I prayed in my mind since I was not able to talk, *Father God, please help me, and let me live.* I even made a vow to God that I would never smoke anything again. After several minutes, my experience was over and so was my attempt of trying to fit in. Once the weekend was over, it was back to Grandma's house and back to school on Monday. My mother had no idea of the things I was doing, and I had no intention of telling her.

My mother would soon find interest in Grandma's neighbor, an older man who was much different from Lehigh. He was an older Hispanic man named Romero, he was 5'7, about 220 pounds, and looked like he worked on a farm. My mother and Romero kept their affection hidden from Brandy and me. I had no idea my mother had been seeing Romero until one day, Lehigh came to New Jersey to visit my mother. I knew it was strange that Romero had not been over Grandma's house in a few days. However, on this particular Wednesday night, Romero came to Grandma's house along with my Aunt Patricia and one of her friends to play cards with my mother, Lehigh, and Uncle Tim. While playing cards, the secret came out. The news of my mother and Romero's relationship caused a big disturbance between Romero and Lehigh, resulting in the police being called to Grandma's house. Grandma was furious and made no apologies for her demeanor when expressing her feelings to my mother about her behavior. Later that night, Lehigh took a train back to South Carolina, and a few days later my mother, Brandy, and I boarded another Greyhound bus headed back to Virginia.

We had no real place to call home. We spent one night at my mother's friend's house and then a week at another one of her friend's houses before we ended up at Ms. Diane's house. Brandy and I were enrolled in school, where we attended for two weeks before Ms. Diane informed my mother she was being evicted from her apartment. My mother had less than one week to find us a new place to stay. My mother called another friend of hers, Ms. Lena, who agreed to let us stay in her apartment. Despite living in Ms. Lena's apartment with six of her family members, I was glad to have a warm place to stay. Brandy and I slept in Ms. Lena's walk-in closet in her living room on a mattress that caused my skin to break out in rashes all over my body. While my mother slept on the couch, she often complained that Ms. Lena's daughter's boyfriend was leaving the apartment all hours of the night, which caused her to get little sleep for work in the morning. It was not the best arrangement, but it was better than being in the cold. My mother enrolled my sister in school, and I stayed home with Ms. Lena since my mother had no transportation to take me to and from my previous school.

One morning while staying home with Ms. Lena, she asked me to wash dishes that were left in the sink from the night before. As I agreed, I looked inside the dishwater and saw several roaches floating at the top of the water. My facial expression had become frowned and frightened. The thought of putting my hands in the cold gray water made me want to instantly spit-up. Ms. Lena noticed my expression, and she assured me when she got her Social Security check, she would buy me an outfit for washing the dishes. Although I didn't want to wash the dishes and I knew that Ms. Lena wasn't going to buy me an outfit. I turned my frown into a smile and remembered that she allowed me, my mother, and Brandy to stay in her home. I put my hands in the cold water to clean out the drain trying not to look at the dead roaches floating around my hand. I prayed to myself, asking God to help my mother find us housing because I could not get used to this type of living. The more the roaches came close to my hand, the harder I prayed, causing Ms. Lena to say, "You ok, baby?" Though I wasn't okay, I just mumbled, "Umm hmm."

Since moving into Ms. Lena's home, I was the new girl in the neighborhood, and it seemed as if all the neighborhood boys wanted to see what I was about. Even Ms. Lena's son, Maxwell, who was two years older than me. Maxwell invited all his neighborhood friends to come to his home, and one by one they asked me several questions mainly about sex. Though I found no interest in their questions or in sex, I just stared at them like I had no idea what they were talking about. After several minutes of getting nowhere, they all left while making jokes about how skinny I was. I just laughed at their jokes, but there was nothing funny about living in an environment that was unstable, not knowing when I was going to eat again, and not knowing when I would see my mother who had not come home to Ms. Lena's the previous night. Later that night, Maxwell sat next to me on the couch as I was watching television. He asked if he could have sex with me. I quickly said, "No!!" as I rolled my eyes in disgust with his question. With my strong reaction Maxwell started laughing, then saying, "Girl, I was just joking with you, why you look like that?" Though it was rough for me living at Ms. Lenas' home, I would never give into the pressure of sex, after all I was a child, just fourteen. Some nights I was not sure if he would try to come into the closet where Brandy and I were sleeping. If he did, it wasn't like my mother was around. I started to become mad with my mother for even allowing me and Brandy to stay in such an environment and then just to leave us. Other nights, I would stay up late to pray and read my Bible. I once read the scripture "Have not I commanded thee? Be strong and of a good courage; be not afraid, neither be thou dismayed: for the LORD thy God is with thee whithersoever thou goest." The Word of God, some nights, would be my meat and potatoes sustaining me through another day.

My mother had started using drugs with Mrs. Hope, one of the women in the neighborhood. There were nights in which my mother would stay overnight at Mrs. Hope's apartment while Brandy and I would go to bed hungry at Ms. Lena's home. My mother had no cell phone to contact her to ask her to bring us food to eat. Ms. Lena's daughters, one night, cooked spaghetti together for their children. The smell of the spaghetti only made me and Brandy even hungrier. However, there was nothing but disappointment for us to eat. They did not share their meal and my mother did not come to Ms. Lena's that night. With no contact with my father, I would hold on to my Faith in God through prayer. I knew God heard me when I prayed. The next day when my mother arrived, I told her that Brandy and I had not eaten the previous night. My mother complained that she purchased food for Brandy and me to eat and insisted Ms. Lena's children had eaten our food. However, there were nine of us living in the three bed-room apartment, so my mother was not sure who ate the food. She also had not been at Ms. Lena's in several nights. My mother discussed a plan to find better housing for us. She then informed me, Lehigh would be moving in the house with us. I was glad to know that my mother had a plan to get us out of Ms. Lena's apartment. I couldn't wait to move.

Within two months, Brandy, Lehigh, my mother, and I moved into a two-bedroom house. It was a small house with a huge backyard. Brandy and I shared a room. We did not have much in our house, my mother had sold all our furniture from our previous apartment. My mother enrolled Brandy and me in school, and my life was beginning to have some sense of stability. I put aside my dislikes for Lehigh. I was just happy to have a home and a comfortable bed to sleep on. My mother maintained her employment at the elementary school, and Lehigh was able to get his previous job back at the local publishing company. I had been enrolled back into my previous school, but there were only three months left in the school term before the summer break. I was concerned I would fail due to being in and out of school and living in two different states. Though it had been a rough and challenging year, I was not going to let it break me. I prayed and asked God to help me pass the eighth grade. I tried my best to get extra credit in some classes. I focused on my schoolwork so that I could pass and sail off to high school. One summer morning, a month after the school year had ended I checked the mail, as usual. I noticed my report card was included in the pile of mail. I rushed into the house, dropping the other mail but holding on to my final report card. I ripped the envelope open as if it was a check, I had passed the eighth grade. I yelled a scream and danced in the middle of the living floor. I felt relieved and sad at the same time. I passed the eighth grade, but Brandy, however, failed the second grade. I blamed my mother for the extra stress Brandy endured moving around from place to place and for not giving her the attention she needed.

That summer, we did not go to Grandma's house in New Jersey. I wasn't even sure if my mother had talked to Grandma since the night the police came to her house. I missed Grandma, Sharell, Michael, and cousin Tameka. I would often think of the fun times we had. These thoughts kept me happy and positive. After four months of living in our new house, I noticed my mother was still using drugs. I always saw my mother's reaction when she was high off cocaine. Her eyes would bulge out of her head, and her mouth would twitch from side to side. Trying to have a conversation with her was impossible, I could not seem to get past her physical appearance. I was so disappointed to see my mother looking this way. Lehigh was also using drugs, his drug of choice was crack cocaine. It was like being in hell all over again. I would pray and ask God to deliver my mother and Lehigh from drugs. Sometimes I felt like God was not listening. Late-night drinking, drug using, and loud music seemed to be my mother's and Lehigh's weekend tradition. Once I remember the music being so loud, it woke me from my sleep. I got out of bed to look for my mother, however, she was nowhere to be found. The side and back door were opened, the front door was unlocked, and all the lights were on. I quickly cut off the music and closed the doors they had left open. I thanked God for covering Brandy and me. We lived in the city, and anything and everything happens in the city. I began crying out to God about my living situation. This could not be my life, it was hard, painful, and unstable. I made it my duty to watch over Brandy and consistently prayed God would make things better and deliver my mother and Lehigh from drugs.

The next Saturday morning, Grandma unexpectedly arrived at our house, with three of my younger cousins, and Uncle Tim. They were on their way to North Carolina to visit my aunts and cousins. Grandma cleared space in her new Chevrolet Astro minivan for Brandy and me, to come along. It would not be long before my mother and Lehigh got dressed to tag along. Lehigh drove his '89 Cadillac Deville, my mother insisted I ride with her and Lehigh; however, I quickly refused, I needed a break from the two of them. It was so good to see Grandma again. I had not seen her in several months. She was jazzy and upbeat as she drove her new minivan. She wore a long, glittered shirt; blue jeans; and sunglasses slightly raised off her nose. She danced in her seat, full of laughter and loud speech. Looking in the rearview mirror at me laughing as she said, "Joi', I am going to get your Aunt Lisa to cook some good food to fatten you up." I just laughed along, quietly thanking God for giving me a break from the dysfunction. She could have said anything, I would still have laughed. I was just glad to be out of the house. For the next two days, I took a mental break. I wanted to ask Grandma if I could live with her while telling her about my mother and Lehigh. However, I knew telling her would be a nightmare waiting to happen. I could see Grandma confronting my mother and Lehigh. My mother would be mad with me, especially if Grandma did not let me live with her. I made the best of my time away, enjoying time with my cousins.

A few weeks later Sharell and Michael visited us in Virginia. Michael had gotten big, he was so cute, and he had the brightest smile. Sharell was not the same. She seemed more experienced with life, and she had plenty of stories to tell me about her interesting life. I enjoyed laughing and talking to my sisters and my mother. It was like old times without financial stress. I wanted to tell Sharell about the dysfunction that was taking place in our home, but I did not want to spoil the good moments we all were having so I kept it all within.

A few days later Sharell and Michael went back to New Jersey and it was back to reality. The new school semester was fast approaching, and there were still no school clothes or school shoes for Brandy and me. I kept asking my mother if she was going to take us to shop for school clothes and shoes. She complained she had no money to take us shopping. She would say, "Call your father and ask him. I know he pays child support, but that little child support check ain't shit." I was so disappointed because I knew the child support checks for Brandy and myself were paying for my mother's and Lehigh's drug habit. Three weeks later, my mother gave Brandy and me sixty dollars to purchase clothes. She told us we could walk to the local plaza to purchase them. Sixty dollars was actually like five dollars. There was only one way to stretch sixty dollars. Buy cheap! I was grateful, I thought, "Let the stretching begin." To my surprise, I was able to purchase one outfit and two shirts. I helped Brandy find appropriate and affordable clothes to wear to school as well. We both had enough money left to buy a sandwich and juice after budget shopping.

Going to the ninth grade was exciting, yet I was still nervous. I did not know what to expect. On the first day of school, I had on my one new outfit, and I managed to style my hair in a French roll. Over the summer months, I managed to learn to do my hair, I had one style though, the French roll. I would use a sock or hair extensions and wrap my hair around to give my French roll a full effect. I made sure I was cute on the first day of school, despite being tall and thin as a rail. I did not look like the average girls in my school, so I had to make sure I always looked my best with what I had. I had one boyfriend that did not mind what I looked like. He would often tell me how pretty I was while walking me to my first class every day. However, after three months of dating, he began talking about sex. Sex was not in any of my schoolbooks so, I decided to end the relationship. Sex was nothing but something to do for most of the horny buzzards, buzzing around the school. It was like all the girls were doing it, and they could not wait to tell their stories. Some of the boys in school could spot out the girls who were not having sex. I went out with two guys my freshman year, and that would soon be the topic for both of them. I refused to be pressured into having sex. I had to press the pause button on the next sophomore guy that asked me out, or maybe God did. Like one of the sophomore guys, named Timothy, who rode my bus. I knew Timothy was watching me from a distance every day. He would just stare at me once I got on the bus to school, trying to see if I would notice him. One day while riding the bus home, Timothy sat next to me. As soon as he sat down, I began to pray in my head. *Lord, please don't let this boy try to talk to me, and most of all, please don't let him look down at my balled up, beat up black high-top Reebok sneakers.* I saw him out of the corner of my eye, smiling as if he thought I was going to look at him, but I didn't. I kept looking out the window like I did not see him sitting next to me. It wasn't long before he got up and went to the back of the bus where he had been sitting. I laughed in my head, thinking to myself, *God, you are amazing, either you or my sneakers scared the boy away.*

Throughout my freshman year, I tried to maintain a positive attitude. I joined the student council group, where I was able to discuss my concerns at home. I used the group as therapy. I needed someone I could talk to and still feel like everything was going to be alright. One day at the group,

I met a girl named Tanesha, who would become one of my best friends. Tanesha discussed the trauma she was experiencing from her mother, who had bipolar disorder. Tanesha explained how her mother had been verbally abusing her. After listening to Tanisha's concerns, I thought my concerns were not so bad. But then I quickly thought, yes, they were because I needed my mother. My mother was starting to become more distant from Brandy and myself. Everything was about Lehigh, who controlled and manipulated her. I knew the only way to reach her was through prayer.

One day, my fifth-period gym teacher, Mr. Stewart, assigned my class to run five laps around the gym as part of our endurance test. After the second lap, my French roll started to come loose. I thought, *Oh no, not right now.* I had three more laps left. Before I could get to the end of the lap, the sock I used to shape my French roll was no longer attached to my hair. A few seconds later, one of the students in my gym class said, "Ay, your white sock back there on the flo'" as he ran past me. Once home, I told my mother what happened. I told her I wanted to look like my peers. I wanted new clothes, new shoes, cute purses, and most of all I wanted my hair done. Lord knows I was getting tired of that French roll. She said, "Joi', I don't have no money to get your hair done. Look at my hair. Shit, I need my hair done too." She began complaining she did not have much money and told me all the monthly bills she and Lehigh had to pay. Her response was very upsetting, and she was starting to get on my nerves. I felt like I had to do something. Frustrated, I went to my friend Brice's house to talk to his mother, Ms. Sharita. I would visit Ms. Sharita to talk about my problems at home. She always listened and offered just a little advice as if she did not want to have any issues with my mother. Sometimes she would change the subject by talking about how proud she was of Brice. Ms. Sharita loved Brice, she had the love for Brice that I wanted my mother to have for me. After my visit, I saw Brice outside playing basketball. I began to tell him about my mother always complaining she did not have any money. I discussed wanting to have nice things like everybody else at school. Brice also complained about not having any money and wanted his own money to buy more clothes and shoes. I was surprised because Brice always had new sneakers and wore the latest clothing. Brice was the only child and was spoiled by Ms. Sharita. Brice was a cool guy, and very popular. He played football and always wanted to look fresh. Brice told me he was talking to one of his friends who sold weed. His friend wanted to put Brice on to it. Brice told me, "Look, if you want to sell some weed, you can sell for me, and I will give you some of the profit." I was thrown off by the offer and was not sure I wanted to go that route for money. I was more so venting like I often do in my peer group. I quickly thought about jail and disappointing my family. Most of all, I was too scared to even try to sell weed. I quickly declined and wished I had not told him anything. I walked away feeling worse than before talking to him.

The next week, after school, I went to my friend Loren's house so she could style my hair. I told my mother and Lehigh I had stayed back after school for a school activity so they would not be expecting me home after school. Loren was my friend from school who always had her hair styled in a cute up-do. Loren told me she could do my hair the same way her hair was styled. However, after she had styled my hair, it looked nothing like the hairstyle she had. Disappointed, I walked to my house, which was six houses from Loren. Lehigh asked me about my hairstyle. He figured out I did not stay after school for an activity, but instead to have my hair done. He told me to go into my room and strip down to my bra and underwear, he was going to whoop me for lying to him. I looked at my mother as though she would object; however, she said nothing. And just like Lehigh stated, he gave me four lashes with his belt in my room. I felt so disrespected that he saw me with hardly any clothes on and my mother said nothing. I thought she was going to stand up for me and just put me on punishment. I soon started to dislike my mother and Lehigh even more. Brandy came into our room and just looked at me as if she had felt my pain. We both discussed wanting to move away from my mother and Lehigh.

I often walked to the local store for snacks. On this particular day, I decided to walk a different way to the store, a longer route than usual. I wanted to have more time out of the house away from my mother and Lehigh. While I was walking, I saw a church in a residential neighborhood. After noticing the church, I soon began visiting the church every week. My mother dropped me off to church every Sunday. Brandy would attend church with me some Sundays. I made sure I was always on time for church. Attending church was my escape from my reality. I knew God was real and attending church was my cry out for help from my home and family challenges. I needed to be around people who prayed and loved God and did not mind showing it. This display of love for God encouraged me and made me want to look past my current family situation. I would attend church only to come home to my mother and Lehigh still using drugs, my mother's distant relationship with me, and still no new clothes or shoes to wear to school. After attending church for a few weeks, I joined the church. It was like the best thing I could have ever done with my life. I received hugs and smiles from the members of the congregation. I felt so hopeful, full of life, and happy. I told Brice about the church service I attended, and I told him I joined the church. Within three weeks, Brice began attending the church and joined as well. Soon, we both signed up to get baptized. You could not tell me anything, I was so excited about my life. I was like sunshine, a beam of never-ending light. I felt good and excited about getting baptized. I called my father, whom I had not spoken to in months and invited him to my baptism service. The day of my baptism, Brice and I were both nervous and happy at the same time. Ms. Sharita was at the church, all dressed up. My mother, Lehigh, and Brandy were also at the church in their finest attire. I was surprised to look out into the congregation to see my father who came to see me get baptized. He had his camera in his hand, ready to take my picture. I was called before Brice. As I went into the water, I just closed my eyes, hoping to go into the cold water and come up with a new mind and a better life. Now that I received salvation and had been baptized, I was expecting God to turn my life around and to have a closer relationship with Him.

I continued to go to church every week and had gained *Favor* with Pastor Rhodes and First Lady Rhodes. They had three children, two were twin boys, David, and Daniel, who were ten months, and their daughter Leah who was five. One night, First Lady Rhodes called me to see if I would be interested in watching their children while they went to an evening conference. I gladly said yes, anything to get out of the house and to make a few dollars to buy some clothes.

The next day when I arrived at their house David, Daniel, and Leah were already in bed. However, David and Daniel were not asleep. I sat with them until they went to sleep, just watching them as they slept. The boys reminded me so much of my little nephew, Michael. Their eyes were greenish blue looking. They had curly brown hair and the softest brown skin. I began to cry and pray for Michael and Sharell, whom I missed so much. I often talked to Sharell and Michael on the phone. However, watching the twins made me want to see them more. After Pastor Rhodes and First Lady Rhodes arrived back home, First Lady Rhodes took me back home and gave me twenty dollars for watching their children. I was so glad to have a few dollars to buy a shirt or socks.

Once home, I went to the bathroom and looked out the window. I noticed in our backyard a car sitting with a light flickering on and off. I quickly woke my mother up to inform her of what I saw. She informed me that it was Lehigh in the car. She told me to go to bed and that everything was okay. I knew that it wasn't. A few hours later, Lehigh would disrupt our home as Brandy and I slept. Lehigh began screaming at my mother to give him "the money," and my mother yelled back that she didn't have any more money. My mother had put the money Lehigh was looking for in my room under my mattress. After enough of him screaming and twisting my mother's arm, she told him where the money was located. Lehigh barged in my room and attempted to take the money from under my mattress. I jumped up and pushed Lehigh's hand from under my mattress before he quickly tossed me onto the floor. My mother screamed, "Joi' give him the money, give him the money." I looked at him in his face and said, "I ain't giving you no money." Lehigh looked for the money under my mattress and did not find it, because I had the money folded up in my hand. Lehigh pushed me, and I pushed him back, and we began to tussle in the middle of the floor. I tried my best not to let go of the money. I thought about this money being my and Brandy's clothes and shoes money. I was not letting up. My mother began pushing Lehigh, saying, "Joi' give him the money, give him the money, give him the money." I was angry, I threw the money at him, and he quickly picked up the money and left our house. I was furious, complaining to my mother that Lehigh's behavior was unacceptable and how low he was for tussling with me for her money to buy drugs. I knew I had to get out of my mother's house because it was not a healthy environment for Brandy or me. I once saw one of my classmates mysteriously at my home, he looked at me and I looked at him. We did not exchange any words, for he had come to deliver drugs to Lehigh. I called my father to ask him if Brandy and I could live with him at Aunt Beth's house. However, he just said, "There is no space for you and Brandy."

The next weekend my father had come to my mother's house to pick up Brandy and me for the weekend, taking us to Aunt's Beth's house where he had been staying. After playing a card game with Aunt Beth, Brandy, and cousin Tina (Aunt Beth's daughter); my father came out of his room, staring at us with his big brown eyes bulging out of his head as if he were going to hit us or attack us. He said, "I thought someone was talking about me." I just stared at him in disbelief and looked away. I soon found out my father was using crack cocaine just like Lehigh. I was so hurt and tired of being let down by my parents. Even though I was saved, baptized, and had been going to church, nothing was getting better for me. I felt like I was going to continue to stay in my current situation. I prayed and cried out to God and complained to God that my life was not fair. I was not sure why I was experiencing the challenges in my life. I felt like God had forgotten about me. I did not want to live with my mother and Lehigh or with my father. The thought of running away seemed like my only option. The thought of suicide was my next option. I thought, maybe my life would be better with God. I heard a small voice telling me to kill myself and that my life was not going to get better. The devil told me to use a razor and cut my wrist. I wrestled with the thought, but I was too afraid. I did not want to die. I soon started to believe my life would get better and that something good was going to come out of my situation. I planned to continue to believe in God. I believed He would help me and make my life better. I just did not know how or when.

Lehigh's sister, Aunt Rose, would often come to our house to visit. She was very supportive and available to me when she was not working. When I had my tap dance recital, she attended. She was my only supporter as I danced to a jazz tune selection. My mother and Lehigh did not attend. Even though I was disappointed, I was glad Aunt Rose was there. She was always pleasant and patient with me. She was also pleasant and patient with her children, Jada, and Riley, who were five and two. She made sure to give Jada and Riley the attention they needed. To me, she was a great example of a mother. On this day, Aunt Rose came to talk to my mother to ask if I could go with her to Miami, a place I had never been to before. I was so excited for the chance to fly on an actual plane, also something I had never done before. I could not wait, I started packing before I heard my mother tell her I could go. I knew she wouldn't say no to Aunt Rose. Aunt Rose told my mother she was meeting her friend, Mr. Samuel, in Miami. Mr. Samuel was someone she met at a concert in the Bahamas. She asked my mother if I could go to Miami to help her with her children, who would be going to Miami too. My mother agreed, and the next week off to Miami, we went.

Miami was a beautiful place. The beach water was bright and full of life. There were so many people. It was so good to see a new place and to be away from home. Mr. Samuel greeted us with a pleasant smile and a hug as he introduced himself to Jada, Riley, and me. We all went to Bayside for lunch. The sounds of the live steel drum band were so relaxing. People with different beautiful skin tones sat outside eating and talking. It was like a whole new free world. A place I was thankful to God to have had the chance to see. We toured the city of Miami on a beautiful longboat where fresh fruit drinks and bite-size foods were served. There were so many houses painted with so many beautiful bright colors. Some of the homes even looked as if they were going up a clustered hill all stacked together. Just being on the boat ride, I felt refreshed and free. I thought about my life one day being different, I imagined how God would make it beautiful.

Two weeks after coming back from Miami, Aunt Rose arrived at my house to tell us that she was relocating to Philadelphia, due to an employment transfer. She planned to find housing in Maryland. I was so sad to hear Aunt Rose was leaving. I felt my one safety net had just been pulled from underneath me. I felt like I had to conquer my situation with God alone. Though my life was tough, I remained focused on my studies. I attended school as scheduled and completed my assignments as instructed. I was doing everything I could do to stay focused while staying positive. Despite the challenges and obstacles, I continued to pray. I believed God that my parents' lives would be changed, and they would be delivered from drugs.

And through all of this, I passed the ninth grade!

DETERMINATION

" I can do all things through Christ which strengtheneth me. "
Philippians 4:13

———————⟨◇⟩———————

In the summer of 1994, Aunt Rose met with my mother at our house. She wanted me to move to Maryland with her, Jada, and Riley. I listened to their conversation as I pretended to watch another episode of Martin. Although I loved watching Martin to laugh over my pain, I would have to watch this episode again. Aunt Rose told my mother that she was renting a three-bedroom house in a quiet residential development. She discussed with my mother the benefits of having me move with her to Maryland. With no thought, my mother refused. I was surprised my mother declined. I quickly ran into the kitchen where they were sitting to remind my mother of the sophomore student who was shot in the stomach while eating lunch in the school cafeteria at my school and how the other students ran through the halls screaming about the incident. I then reminded her of the time a male student in my math class exposed himself to me. I dug up every reason why my mother should let me move to Maryland. Although I did not know what I was getting myself into, I was determined to give it a try. Besides, my mother and I did not have a real mother and daughter relationship. She did not talk much to Brandy or me, she was more concerned about pleasing Lehigh. I was losing respect for her, especially after she allowed Lehigh to give me a whooping with just my underclothes on. I was ready for a new beginning and to be let loose from the chains of lack, dysfunction, and fear. I was ready for a new life and a stable environment, where I could be a teenager with no worries. A week later, my mother finally approved of me going to live in Maryland with Aunt Rose. I was so excited. I remember telling Brandy as we instantly hugged. I know my mother would not have allowed Brandy to go if Aunt Rose had asked her. My mother would have probably felt alone, with all her children no longer living with her. I told Brandy I would call her as often as I could just to make sure that she was okay. I was sad to leave Brandy, for we used to lay in our beds and make jokes while laughing hysterically. We found that humor helped drown out our problems at home. It was either humor or music, sometimes both. I would miss the dance routines we made to Xscape's, "Just Kickin' It," or Tag Team's, "Whoomp There It Is" or Salt-N-Pepa's, "Shoop." I wanted Brandy to hold on to the memories of the fun we had because I knew she would have to deal with Lehigh on her own. Although my mother had stopped using drugs, Lehigh continued. To my surprise, Brandy did not seem as sad as I thought she would. She did not even seem to mind.

I loved my new home. The neighborhood was well kept. The house was spacious, and most of all I had a room for myself. Although I never minded sharing a room with Brandy, I was glad to have a space designated just for me to be alone. As often as I wished, I now thanked God almost every day for a new change of environment and a better life. I was glad to have a stable, steady, and healthy living environment. To show my appreciation, I always kept my room clean, my bed made, and my new room filled with sunshine. The sunshine made me feel happy, and it gave me a feeling of comfort.

In the first month of living with Aunt Rose, she had taken Jada, Riley, and me to Sesame Place in Pennsylvania. Though it was too kidlike for me, I was glad to see new places and to see people as happy as I was. I admired the way Aunt Rose loved her children and showed her love for them. Even when they whined and cried, she managed to keep her composure, even when she wanted to scream. She tolerated their behavior so well, something I would soon learn to do as well. The next week Aunt Rose took me shopping for school, which was a few weeks away. Aunt Rose had already enrolled me in school. She was always on top of things. She took me to King of Prussia mall to purchase several outfits, a pair of dress shoes, and a pair of Nike sneakers. Though this was normal for some girls my age, this was anything but ordinary for me. I felt a little sad though because I knew Brandy probably would not get much for school. I prayed to God that He would allow my mother to purchase Brandy cute clothes and up to date shoes. I thought it would be easier since my mother only had to buy clothes for Brandy.

On my first day of high school as a sophomore, it was an extreme culture shock experience. At my new school, there were about fifty Black students, maybe twenty Asian and Hispanic students combined, and the rest of the hundreds of students were White. I was from the inner city where there were predominantly Black students in my school, with maybe fifteen White students, ten Hispanic students, and there were no Asian students. The first thing I thought about was segregation, Martin Luther King Jr., and racism. I even heard white students in the halls at school, making jokes about the Black students using hair grease. I saw some of the Black students huddled together at the side door in the upstairs foyer. Some of the White students were also gathered together by the office and the cafeteria. The Hispanic and Asian students were gathered in the cafeteria as well. Some other blended groups of students were also in the cafeteria before class began. I had to find my place as the new girl in school quickly. I was tall and still thin as a rail. I did not smile because most of the students did not look friendly. I noticed how some of the girls that looked like me would stare at me during my first couple of months at school, looking to see what I was wearing. I heard one of them say, "Damn, she is skinny," as they all laughed together. I made an instant eye connection before walking to my class, thinking *Lord not here too*, this was my new start.

One month after starting school, while sleeping, Aunt Rose had awakened me to receive a phone call from Grandma. Once on the phone, Grandma spoke in a soft voice. She said, "Joi' I have some bad news to tell you." My heart started beating ten times faster. She said, "Sharell died today. She was in a fight with someone, and they stabbed her and pierced her heart, and she died while at the hospital. Aunt Rose is going to bring you to my house in a few days, and I will be here when you arrive." Shocked and confused, I simply said, "Okay." My heart felt like it stopped beating, and I just sat on Aunt Rose's bed frozen. I did not know what to do or say, other than "Lord why, she was only eighteen?" Aunt Rose hugged me as I cried, wondering how Michael was doing and how his life was going to be without his mother. I went to bed, and the next morning I was still in disbelief. I prayed throughout the day as I tried to focus on my class assignment throughout my day at school.

When I arrived at Grandma's house, I saw my cousins and Sharell's boyfriend standing in the front yard. They were all standing around talking. I didn't speak, I just wanted to see Grandma. I went into Grandma's house to find her and hug her, for she was my comforter. I saw my mother, Brandy, and Michael, whom I hugged so tightly, closing my eyes, wishing this were all a dream. I saw my father, whom I had not seen in several months, he held me while crying.

He kept saying, "Please call me sometime." This was a sad and hard time for my family and me. After the funeral, we talked about the good times with Sharell, and that is how I planned to remember her. Michael moved to Virginia with my mother, Brandy, and Lehigh. My father and Uncle Glenn went back to Virginia as well. I went back to Maryland, and my routine continued, with no time to grieve.

I was determined to stay focused on my studies and pass my classes, despite the never-ending challenges I continued to endure. I believed and always had Faith that "I can do all things through Christ which strengtheneth me." With scars and bruises, I planned to do something my mother nor Sharell ever did, which was finish high school.

During my first semester of school, I met Natasha, who lived in my housing development. She was my first real friend. Natasha lived with both her parents and her sister Mia in one of the bigger houses in the development. Natasha's parents were very protective. They always had Natasha and Mia's best interest in mind and made sure they had the best. I loved going over to Natasha's spacious and consistently clean house. Natasha was very cool and very down to earth. I felt like I knew her my whole life. We would laugh all the time about the silliest things or make unthought-of jokes and even jokes about our peers at school. This was the type of laughter I needed my whole life. We would do the oddest things. Once, we went to view a house for sale in a new development with a realtor. Natasha and I followed the realtor all around the new wall to wall carpeted, freshly painted home. We made finger signs behind his head as we walked down to the basement. We were laughing so hard while the realtor described the features of the house. Once, he even laughed with us as if he knew what we were laughing at, which made Natasha and I laugh even more. Before he could tell us about the square footage of the basement and all its bells and whistles, I saw water coming from Natasha's pants. Natasha had laughed so hard she had peed her pants. Natasha quickly said, "Thank You, Sir, the house is beautiful, but we have to leave." With no indication of what had happened, the realtor thanked us for viewing the new house as we laughed, running up the steps. I just hoped he had a carpet cleaner somewhere in the house, for he would soon need it.

In the middle of the school year, I was struggling with my transition. I felt like I had enrolled in college. The quality of education was at a higher standard than what I was used to. My classes were challenging, which made me work harder. I made sure to stay focused on my grades. I also struggled at times with acceptance. I had been taken out of the city and had moved into a suburb where my peers talked differently and dressed differently from me. Most of the students in the school were not concerned about designer clothes and up-to-date shoes. They seemed to just wear what they had. They were just fine with their appearance, which was unlike what I was used to. I also met some students who had more than the average student had. They sometimes looked down on the other students. I could spot them out easily since they all dressed and talked alike and had their noses so far in the air, they could smell Jesus. I often called them the "nobodies." I started listening to alternative rock bands like Oasis, No Doubt, The Smashing Pumpkins, and The Cranberries, just to name a few. I had opened myself up to new experiences. An experience I was not used to. It was so different, not the ordinary, and definitely nothing I had experienced.

While Aunt Rose worked, after school, I had the responsibility of picking up Jada and Riley from their daycare provider in our development. Once we were home, I helped Riley with his homework, prepared dinner for us to eat, made sure they had taken a bath before putting Jada and Riley to bed. It was exhausting at times. I had to make time to study and complete my massive homework assignments. I felt like I was a student and a mother at the same time, at the age of sixteen. Though I was thankful to God for the well-needed change in my life, I was starting to think this change was coming with a price. There were times I was not able to attend basketball or football games due to Aunt Rose's work schedule. I had to care for Jada and Riley. I often thought, 'what have I done, and maybe I should tell Aunt Rose I wanted to go back home. I felt alone all over again. Despite my feelings, this time, I had to stay strong for two small people instead of just one, which was Brandy. I had so much responsibility for passing my classes and caring for Jada and Riley. I prayed every day, asking God to help me and to give me the strength to endure. I was determined to get through my struggles and challenges with my new transition.

Though my academics were challenging at times, and I was still trying to find my identity, I was also struggling with insecurity issues that stemmed from my childhood. I never felt good enough, or pretty enough, which made it hard for me to feel accepted. I always wanted to feel accepted. Though this feeling started as a child, it had now trickled into my adolescent years. I would often complain to God, who had become my best friend besides Natasha, about my weight, and that I needed to gain weight. I was tired of being skinny. I complained that I had to wear two pairs of pants to school so that I could fill out my pants.

I remember hanging out with my friends from school. We had piled up together in one car and went to the Christiana Mall to eye shop, which was shopping with our eyes and without actual money. While shopping with my friends we noticed a group of cute tall guys, who looked like they played high school basketball, walking towards us. We began straightening our clothes and hair, perfecting ourselves for their approach. As they came near, the tallest guy out of the bunch asked me for my name. Too shy to turn around, I just walked past him. He soon approached me and directly asked me for my name and phone number. I thought out of all these girls, I was the lucky pick. I provided him with my name and phone number. Although I was happy at the time, I still struggled with this insecurity that would linger throughout high school. I joked around a lot and appeared to be happy with who I was, but I was very insecure. I was often surprised when someone wanted to go out with me or even ask for my phone number because of my insecurities. I never let my friends know I was too ashamed to discuss my childhood. I pretended as if I knew Leon would approach me, as my friends questioned when I was going to call him. I felt like God was saying you are beautiful, just the way you are. I believed God had a sense of humor.

After hard work and prayer, I made it through my sophomore year and passed to the eleventh grade. I went home to Virginia for the summer. I was so glad to see my mother, Brandy, and Michael, who had grown taller since I last saw him. This was the first time I had seen my family since Sharell's funeral. I hugged Brandy and Michael so tightly as if I had not seen them in years. I was so glad to see Brandy. She looked the same, still tall, and skinny. We instantly spent time catching up on our time away from each other. I shared with her my experience in Maryland, and she shared what had been happening at home with my mother and Lehigh. I called Brandy throughout the school year. She never said much other than, "I'm okay." However, while I was home for the summer, I was able to talk to her to find out how she had been. I was glad to see my mother, and I even talked often to Lehigh. I told my mother about my time at Aunt Rose's house and let my mother and Brandy listen to some of the alternative rock music I started listening to. My mother quickly objected. She said, "Oh no turn that white people shit off. We don't listen to that. You moved to Maryland and turned white." Though I just laughed, I realized my mother had a lot to learn, and sometimes you must get out of your comfort zone to learn. My mother tried to rekindle our relationship. I guess she missed me while I was away at school. However, Lehigh always managed to steal away her efforts by finding something else to focus her attention on.

Almost every morning I would go outside in the backyard with Michael to play. Sometimes, he would look up at the sky while pointing his little finger, and tell me, "My mommy is up there." Trying not to cry, I would agree, often saying, "Yep, you're right, your mommy is in Heaven with God." I often blamed my mother for my sister's death, thinking if she had never sent Sharell to New Jersey, her death would not have happened. I had a conversation with my mother one day about my concern. She quickly yelled at me, saying, "It was not my fault." To my surprise, I began yelling back at her, resulting in a shouting match between the two of us. Lehigh ran in the living room from the kitchen and grabbed my mother, who was trying to hit me. I was so angry I could not wait to go back to Aunt Rose's house. If I thought by chance, my relationship with my mother was going to get better, this argument shot down that opportunity. For the rest of the summer, I made sure to spend time with Brandy and Michael and to stay out of my mother's way. We barely talked or did anything together. I found myself back at Ms. Sharita's house to discuss my concerns about my mother before she would begin talking about Brice. Within a few weeks, Aunt Rose arrived in Virginia to take me back to Maryland so I could begin my next school year.

During my junior year, I was used to the routine of attending school and picking up Jada and Riley from their daycare provider. This year Jada was now in school, so I had the responsibility of helping her and Riley with their homework along with the rest of the evening tasks. I knew what to expect, and without any complaining to God, I did what was expected of me. Although I did not complain, I was looking for a break from my routine. I started to take an interest in some of the boys at school, I didn't discriminate, and that meant I was verbally involved with some of the black guys at school and the white guys as well. Once, I hung out with a white guy named John who had graduated the school year before. I was attracted to him since my sophomore year of school, but to my surprise, he had a girlfriend. After he graduated, they must have broken up because he gave his phone number to his sister to give to me. This was my first time hanging out with a white guy and, though he was white, I did not see his skin color. The first time we went to the park where we found the oddest things to talk about and the second time he came to my house, both times he looked for something I was not willing to give. Though I was attracted to John, I made sure to ignore his calls. I was not willing to give away my pearls.

One day, Mr. Samuel came to our house to visit Aunt Rose for one week. I had not seen him since our trip to Miami; however, I was so glad he arrived. I did not know what to do, whether to dance, sing, or shout because break time was in session for me. Aunt Rose had taken off work for five days of his seven-day visit and, on those days, I made sure to hang out with my friends after school. Aunt Rose never questioned me when I arrived back home. She had given me a time to be back home, and I honored her request. My friends had their cars, and they would meet at my house. We would pile up in one car and go to parties in Delaware filled with alcohol, plenty of cute guys, and loud music. I felt like I was with my cousin Tameka and her friends in New Jersey. No one was dancing when we first entered the house party as A Tribe Called Quest's "Stressed Out" played. Everyone was standing on the wall sipping from their red cups. I thought, 'what kind of party is this?'; as for my friends and me, we just looked at each other thinking we should leave. However, as soon as Busta Rhymes, "Woo Hah" played, it was like an altar call. Everybody was jumping around and dancing. From then, the party was hype, and so was I. I danced, laughed, and had a tad bit to drink before returning home. Once back home, I saw Aunt Rose interacting with Mr. Samuel. She was so happy, staring at him as he talked; she looked as if she was in love. Mr. Samuel was a handsome man. He was from the Caribbean island of Saint Lucia. He always looked and smelled as if he was going out on a date. He would always tell me I needed to gain weight as if I did not already know. I just would say, "Yeah, I know," as I rolled my eyes. Mr. Samuel did not talk much except when we would go out for fun or the time when we went to Philadelphia to see some of the historic museums. He then spoke about Saint Lucia and some of his cultural traditions. He even prepared some of his traditional meals from his island which he assured if I ate daily would make me gain weight. After Mr. Samuel left to go back to Saint Lucia, Aunt Rose went back to work, and I was back to my routine of taking care of Jada and Riley. One evening, while I was listening to the Fugees, "Ready or Not," dancing and singing away in my room as if I had an audience. Aunt Rose came into my room and, with a soft tone, she told me that she was pregnant. I was surprised. Though I was excited for Aunt Rose, I knew this would be more responsibility for me. However, despite knowing the baby would be coming, I continued to stay focused on my studies. I prayed to God that He would help me and give me the strength to endure more responsibility.

The next Sunday Aunt Rose took Jada, Riley, and me to a church in Delaware. At the end of the service, the Pastor asked people in the large congregation to come to the altar if they wanted to be filled with the Holy Spirit. Though I wanted to be filled with the Holy Spirit, I was afraid to go to the altar. My heart was beating extra fast, and I felt like everyone was looking at me. Still fearful, I took the bit of courage I had with me to the altar to be filled with the Holy Spirit. There were about ten people at the altar, including me. The Pastor said a prayer, we repeated the prayer, and then praised God. Soon after praising God, I began speaking in tongues. I had never heard of speaking in tongues, nor had I ever spoken in tongues before. But that morning I felt the power of God. This experience left me knowing, if I prayed to God asking of Him anything that was in His will for my life in the name of Jesus and praised Him for it, I would have it. I went back to my seat thinking, 'God you are so awesome, despite every trial, situation, and obstacle life brings.'

While in school, God allowed me to meet and befriend students who were experiencing life's challenges as I was. Some of the students looked like me, and other students did not. I was shocked to know that they were using drugs or had resulted in starving themselves. Before attending this school, I had never known about or seen anorexic kids my age nor would I have thought some of the students were using hard drugs like what my mother, Lehigh, and my father used to cope with their challenges in life. I started to believe God allowed me to meet them so that I could see where I could have been if I did not know Him. I was shocked because some of the students were very intelligent and intellectual. Although I felt like my problems were worse than theirs, I thanked God, He kept me. I could have gone another way. I also started to believe my move to Maryland was to open my eyes to a whole new world.

I went to Virginia for the summer after my Junior year. Once arriving home, Brandy and Michael could not wait for me to open the car door to pass out hugs and kisses. My mother seemed happy to see me as well, as she kissed my ear mistaken it for my cheek. Lehigh just waved as he walked past me, heading to his car. Once entering the house, I noticed that Lehigh's three kids were also at our house and, to my surprise, they were living there too. The six of us would share one room. Though I would not have any privacy and there would be nights of sleeping in a tight space, I just told myself it was only for the summer. Most of all, I was glad to be home with Brandy and Michael, whom I had missed while away in Maryland. Brandy and I would think of the funniest things to laugh at and often made jokes about my mother and Lehigh to distract the dysfunction that seemed to plague our home.

I was glad to spend time with Michael, who only wanted to watch DuckTales while telling me about the characters in the cartoon. It would not be long before Lehigh instructed us all to go outside to play, while my mother just sat on the couch. Some days I hated being home for the summer, just the sound of Lehigh's voice always made me want to pack my suitcase and go back to Maryland. I tried to always make the best of my time, by making fun times and when I could not take it no more, I prayed. I then called my father, asking him to pick up Brandy and I for the weekend.

My father was still living with Aunt Beth. He had made Aunt Beth's den his permanent tight living quarters. I always wondered how he could be so comfortable in such a small space, not wanting more for himself, like his own apartment. He had been living in Aunt Beth's house since I was in middle school. I was now a year away from graduating high school. I guess with the look on my face, my father began discussing his plans of moving out of Aunt Beth's house. He told me how he was trying to get his life in order, explaining his past drug use and the events in his life that caused him to begin using crack cocaine. He would laugh as he discussed some of the delusions he remembered while he was high. He told me about a dream he had about an elephant chasing him after he had eaten a pork roll sandwich he found in the refrigerator while he was high and hungry. He told me he woke up staring at the ceiling as he yelled upstairs, asking Aunt Beth to come downstairs to save him. He said she immediately replied, "Boy, go back to sleep." My father and I laughed at his stories, as Brandy played upstairs with Tina. I was glad she was not a part of our conversation, I did not want her to hear or know about my father's drug use. My father talked with me as though I was someone, he could confide in. He discussed attending church and establishing his relationship with God again. I was proud of my father for his transparency and for the necessary steps he was taking to maintain his sobriety and relationship with God. Before my father took Brandy and me back to my mother's house, he told me to always remain humble no matter how much you have achieved or think you have achieved in life. He said, "I see that you moved to Maryland, and now you are starting to think you are better than us, you talking real proper and acting like you forgot where you came from, but stay humble. God moved you away so that you can see that better is out there in life, but baby, please stay humble." I was about to object, thinking, 'who does he think he is talking too,' but I kept quiet because, in all honesty, he was right. I had started looking down on my parents, because of where they were in life, and the accomplishments and the goals they set out but did not obtain compared to my friend's parents.

During my senior year of high school, I enrolled in a Nursing Assistant course at the vocational school while attending my final three classes of high school. After school, I cared for Jada, Riley, and now Aunt Rose's new baby, Jordan, while she worked. I hated carrying Jordan while making sure Jada and Riley kept up during our walk home from their daycare provider's house. Aunt Rose had an '89

Honda Accord in the driveway. I soon started driving to pick up Jada, Riley, and Jordan despite not having a license. I frequently prayed, *'Lord, please keep me, and please do not let me get caught.'* I drove because I grew tired of walking to pick up the kids. Aunt Rose soon allowed me to drive the car that I had already been driving to pick up the kids. That inch she had given me would quickly become a yard. I was now driving to school, to the store, to the mall, and I even drove some of my friends to school. Once I got in the car, I always said my driving prayer, *'Lord, please keep me, and please do not let me get caught driving.'* I never did get caught. I also made sure to focus on my studies and to show Aunt Rose that I was responsible enough to drive while maintaining her trust. Once, she left me home for the weekend while she went to Virginia with Jada, Riley, and Jordan. I partied with my friends Tisha, Taliyah, and Frances all weekend. We were in Maryland then Delaware and back to Maryland in the Honda. We stayed out late and woke up late, I made sure I had fun that weekend knowing that once the weekend was over it would be back to the routine of school and caring for the kids.

I was attracted and talked to several guys throughout high school. I even went out with a handful of them, but I had never met anyone like Justin. He was intelligent, patient, kind, and someone I grew to love. We started dating our senior year of high school. He was my first real boyfriend. I often struggled with my insecurities, which sometimes caused problems in our relationship. Although I made it difficult at times, Justin was patient with me. He would take me out after school and on the weekends whenever Aunt Rose was not working. Though I was dating Justin, I was also talking to Carl, who lived in Delaware. Carl was very handsome and mature looking in stature. He had graduated high school and was attending the local Community College. Carl was always laughing, which was how we met at work, a survey call center. Carl started making jokes about our supervisor. When he noticed my laugh, he took the opportunity to ask me out, and I agreed. Yet Carl had nothing but sex on his mind behind all those midnight jokes he told while talking on the phone. Despite this, I decided to hang out with him on a day Justin unexpectedly came over to my house. I happened to look out the window waiting for Carl to arrive to take me out and, shockingly, I saw Justin getting out of the car. I quickly gathered my purse and told Aunt Rose what was happening. I could hear her laughing as I panicked, she was laughing as if I had told her the funniest joke. She said, "You better get out here, I don't want no ruckus at my house," as she sat on the couch, continuing to laugh. I quickly met Justin at the door. I told him I was hungry, and I needed him to take me to get something to eat. Justin did not ask any questions. He just got in his car to take me to McDonald's. On our way out of my development, I saw Carl entering the development. I'll never forget, he had on black sunglasses and a white shirt. Even though he never saw me, that was the last time I saw

Carl. I was too embarrassed to accept his phone calls or return them. I did not want to explain to him what happened. I later thanked God for Justin because only God would have known what might have happened if I would have gone out with Carl.

In the middle of my senior semester, I went to Brooklyn with one of my best friend's Tisha. Tisha was from Brooklyn. She was fun to be around, and she was the kind of person that no matter what was thrown her way she never ducked to dodge it. She took the shot, sometimes with no emotion. We hopped on the Peter Pan bus and went to Brooklyn to visit her Grandma. Ms. Gray was vibrant and full of life for her older age of sixty-two. She instantly made me feel a part of her family. Every day she told Tisha and me to be careful as we headed out to explore the city. The first night in the city, I quickly adapted to my environment after watching Tisha as we rode the crowded train to get pizza and visit her sister, Lisa. She wore her headphones and said nothing to anybody. I had never taken a train before I visited New York. There were all types of people on the train; some that rapped, some that sang, some that asked for change, and some that even slept. I found myself staring at the people sleeping, wondering if they had missed their stop. Tisha just looked at me laughing because she knew I had never seen so much action. The next day, I made sure to have my headphones on, blasting songs from Tupac's "Machiavelli" and Jay-Z's "Reasonable Doubt" to keep up with Tisha, who seemed to have on Megatron sneakers that made her walk super-fast. I often adjusted my face to a mean expression, like Tisha, so that no one would say anything to me. The previous night all I heard was, "Ay yo slim, slim with the white coat on." Not tonight or the next night, I made sure to blast the head-bobbing lyrics of my two favorite rappers that filled my ears. I also made sure to keep up with Tisha as we walked through the streets and through the massive crowds of people who seemed like they were paid by the city to hang outside in the cold. New York was loud and very cold. My feet felt like they had become frostbitten by all the snow we walked through. But like Tisha, I could not show it. We took the train to Manhattan to shop, there were all types of stores to buy from. I felt like I was in heaven. I bought my first name plated gold necklace that I rocked on Monday morning once I returned to school. I felt like I had made it big with my gold chain. And, I had been to New York City. I just knew I was the coolest. I could not wait to tell my friends about my experience and my time exploring the city.

Though my senior year was ending in less than five months, I had passed my Nursing Assistant class. And I started my nursing clinicals at the local hospital. I had the duty of assisting patients who needed help with their daily needs, I completed blood pressure checks, and recorded vital signs of existing patients. I drove myself to the hospital, back to school, and to pick up Jada, Riley, and Jordan before starting our evening routine. One time, after leaving the hospital, a police officer followed me back to school. I prayed my one-line driving prayer as I was extra careful to follow the speed limit and traffic signs. Once I arrived at school and parked the car in the student's parking lot, I jumped out of the car and began thanking God during my run to my class. I knew I had to get my license, I believed *God's Grace* might have been getting very slim. I practiced for my driving permit, and I passed my first try. I then completed a driving course which my father paid for. I failed my driving test the first time. However, the second time Natasha's father went with me to the Department of Motor Vehicles. He even helped me practice parallel parking before my driving test, which was the reason I had failed the test. After taking the driving test the second time, I was relieved to have passed.

As Senior year was coming to an end, prom season was quickly approaching. Justin and I went to prom together with Tisha and Shawn. I wore my silver and black dress with a pair of blue jean shorts underneath to give me a little shape in my dress. Justin wore a black and white tuxedo. Though we did not match, you couldn't tell us anything. We were the perfect prom King and Queen. We were the perfect number ten, I was the tall, slender one and Justin the shorter zero. Despite our height and weight difference, Justin and I made our prom night fun. It was epic, it was classy; and Justin and I stayed out all night. The next morning once I arrived home, I created a story of my night out on the beach with some friends where we hung out until dawn. Even though Aunt Rose knew I was not telling the truth, she did not say anything more about my prom night.

In June 1997, I graduated from Elkton High School. On the day of my high school graduation, my father and Uncle Glenn arrived at Aunt Rose's house together, followed by my mother, Lehigh, Michael, and Brandy. I was so happy to have my family and friends from high school, attending my graduation. Once my name was called at graduation, I heard my family cheering and yelling my name as I walked across the stage to receive two diplomas, one for completing the Nursing Assistant program and the other for completing high school. I was cheering for myself in my head like, 'You did it, girl, you go girl.' My graduation would be one of the happiest days of my life. Through the years of persevering through the raging storms, I stayed determined to let nothing stop me from accomplishing my goals. Though it was hard and sometimes painful, God was with me every step of the way. He allowed some things, and He kept me through all things. After my graduation dinner, my family headed back to Virginia. Within a week, I was on the Peter Pan bus to Brooklyn with Tisha.

FAITH

"So then faith cometh by hearing, and hearing by the word of God."
Romans 10:17

———————◇◇◇———————

I stayed in Brooklyn with Tisha for one month before running out of money and moving back to my mother's house in Virginia. My mother had moved from the two-bedroom house and had purchased a three-bedroom house. The house was a mid-size rancher with plenty of backyard space, a spacious upgrade from the last house we had lived in. After my arrival, I had a conversation with my mother about attending college and the money she had saved for me. I wanted to go off to college like the rest of my peers, whose parents had saved money for their college expenses. My mother responded by saying, "If you want to go to college, you have to pay for it. It's for you, right?" She said, "I didn't save money for you to go to college, I had bills I had to pay and with what was I supposed to save?" Disgusted by her response, I soon knew if I wanted to go to college, I was on my own. I figured my mother did not have money for college, because she may have used her money to purchase drugs for her and Lehigh. The next week I applied to attend classes at J. Sargeant Reynolds Community College, and I also applied for financial aid. I soon realized if I wanted anything in life, I had to continue to believe God by Faith while taking the steps needed to accomplish my goals.

One month after being in Virginia, I started my first job as a full time Certified Nursing Assistant. The work was hard yet rewarding. My mother would take me to work by six in the morning and pick me up at three-thirty in the afternoon. I worked with older women who were CNAs, that probably came with the building. They believed they controlled the unit. They knew which patients they wanted to work with and which patients they wanted the other CNAs to work with, despite the nursing assignment. They had worked at the Assisted Living Facility for over twenty years, and I was the new person. There was no way that I was making any changes to their already established system. I was assigned ten patients. Seven of the patients could not bathe or dress themselves. I had to lift them to wash them, put on their clothing, comb or brush their hair, brush their teeth if they had any, and sometimes feed them if they wanted to eat breakfast and lunch. After one week, I thought I was going to break my back. I only weighed about one hundred and ten pounds. I also had a young patient that was my age. On my first day at work, he discussed why he was a resident of the Assisted Living Facility. He told me that he used to sell drugs and the boys he was selling to tried to rob him and had shot him several times. One bullet hit his spine, which caused him to become paralyzed. He told me he knew the boys who tried to rob him and had once considered them to be his friends. He told me his life story. After listening to his story, I felt heavy and drained. My eyes were also opened to see that life is precious and that I had to make the right decisions with God's help. I was now living back in the city, unlike the suburbs I had grown used to.

Though I had started work, I could not wait to get back home to Michael and Brandy, I missed my sister and nephew. I would help Michael with his homework, and then play UNO with him and Brandy before dinner. My mother made food, but I did not eat neck bones and potatoes, or hamburger helper, or salmon out of the can with rice, or pig feet and macaroni and cheese she often cooked. I remember once telling my mother, "I do not eat the food you like, and I don't eat pork or beef." She seemed not to like my response. Without hesitation, she said, "As long as you are in my house, you eat what we eat, or you buy your food." I knew I had to wait another week before I received my first paycheck, so for several nights, peanut butter and jelly was my dinner of choice. I knew I would not be staying at my mother's house for long; I did not like her attitude towards me. She would often say, "You will never be better than me because you came from me, and you can never be better than where you came from." Though she was putting me down, I tried to pay her no mind and made the best of my time living in her house. Brandy and I would stay up late and make jokes about my mother and Lehigh laughing hysterically as we laid in bed. Laughter always made me feel happy. It just made all the stress of life disappear, it was my natural high. Brandy and I would catch up on the things we had missed while we were away from each other. She would say, "Damn girl, you sound white maine, where did Aunt Rose have you living at?" before we would begin laughing. Though Virginia is not the south to me, many people used a lot of slang, or cut off syllables in words, unlike me. I did not speak much slang and made sure to pronounce every syllable.

While home, I observed how Lehigh walked around the house as if he made it, controlling what was said and done by my mother, Brandy, and Michael. He made the rules and walked around the house like a jail warden always on the post, trying to intimidate and to see who was not following his rules. One afternoon, Lehigh became upset with Brandy for not washing the dishes. He yelled her name as he stood in the kitchen. When she had come into the kitchen to meet him, he pushed her back into the cabinet and demanded to know why she had not washed the dishes. She continued to say, "You are hurting my back, can you please let me go?" I entered the kitchen to see what was going on. My mother sat at the table, smoking a cigarette just watching as if she was watching her favorite television show. I quickly pulled Lehigh's hands off Brandy's shirt, and I told him, "Don't put your hands on Brandy, she told you, you are hurting her back." Before he could say anything, my mother leaped from the table telling me, "Oh no Joi', I got it, I got it." Brandy went into the bathroom crying as I went behind her, but not before looking back at my mother and Lehigh in disgrace. I could not believe my mother. My mind quickly went back to the scuffle between Lehigh and me when he took her money to buy drugs or the time, she allowed him to whoop me. Later that night, I tried to discuss Lehigh's behavior with my mother, which she refused to address. Lehigh entered the kitchen, acting like he was looking out of the dark window, making his presence known. My mother did not say a word. It was as if she had become scared of him. I had never known my mother to be afraid of Lehigh, but at this moment, I could see she had changed. I often asked my sister if Lehigh had hit my mother before, but Brandy never answered me.

A week later, my mother mentioned the need for me to help with the household expenses. She told me I had to pay her fifty dollars a month, and I had to purchase food and toiletries. She also told me I needed to give her money for gas, for taking me to and from work. She gave me a curfew and a list of rules I needed to follow while living in her house. I knew this was Lehigh's doing. I told my mother I would purchase my food, I would follow her rules and give her money for gas. I refused, however, to give her money for staying in her residence. I thought how dare she make me pay her for staying in her house, I just started working. I thought, '*She did not save money for me to go to college, but she wants me to pay her rent?*' However, within three weeks, I started giving my mother the money she requested.

I knew I had to be respectful to my mother, despite how I felt about her actions. She was still my mother. All I could do was pray for Lehigh because I refused to waste any energy on him.

January 1998, I started Community College full time and reduced my hours to part-time at the Assisted Living Facility. I felt so responsible and I felt like I was on the right path to success. Valentine's Day was one month away, Justin and I had been continuing our long-distance relationship. We were making plans for Valentine's Day weekend. Justin planned to drive to Virginia to pick me up and head back to Maryland together, and then drive me back to Virginia. While on the phone with him, I had gotten caught up in my conversation and forgot the house warden Lehigh was on duty. Lehigh came into the dark kitchen and saw that I was on the phone past my eleven o'clock curfew. He told me to get off the phone and placed me on restriction for being on the phone past curfew. I was furious that he put me on restriction. Just the sound of his voice telling me I was on restriction made me dislike him even more.

The next day my mother took me to work, and we had the conversation about Lehigh putting me on restriction. I told my mother, "I hope he takes me off restriction before Valentine's Day," she gave me a look like "Yeah right." Her facial expression made me wonder if Lehigh was going to take me off restriction in time. I began feeling stressed, however I continued my day at work, trying to avoid any extra conversations with the women at work. After work, I went to class. I was not able to focus on my two classes, but I managed to pull through to complete my in-class assignments before going home. Arriving home after school and work was stressful for me. However, once I was home, Lehigh seemed as if he was happy with my misery of being on restriction as he walked through the house.

Valentine's Day was two days away. I asked my mother and Lehigh when I would be off restriction since I had plans to go to Maryland with Justin. Lehigh told me I would not be going to Maryland and I would be staying home with Michael and Brandy while he and my mother went out for Valentine's Day. I was laughing inside in total disbelief. He thought I was going to stay home while he and my mother went out for Valentine's Day. Now knowing Lehigh's plan, I then revamped my plan, and on Valentine's Day, I did not go to work. I waited until Lehigh left the house and my mother went to work, before calling Aunt Beth to inform her of the events that led up to my plan to leave my mother's house. I asked her if I could stay with her, and to my surprise, she agreed. I called Justin and told him to come and get me. I told him my plans of moving with Aunt Beth. I told Brandy about my plans, as well. This was yet another time I would be leaving her. She said, "Girl, I get it, I would leave too," as she smiled and hugged me. Later that day, Justin came to my mother's house to pick me up. Lehigh had not arrived home and my mother was still at work. Justin and I loaded up his car with my bags of clothes and suitcase. I told Michael I was moving and planned to come and visit him. I only imagined what he was thinking in his five-year-old mind as he just hugged me while I waited for my mother and Lehigh to arrive back home. After ten minutes of waiting, Brandy told me, "Girl, you better leave before they get back because it's going to be on and poppin if you stay and wait for them." Brandy, at fourteen years old, was so much wiser than me in some areas, and this was one of those areas. I kissed Brandy and Michael and headed to Aunt Beth's house to drop off my clothes and suitcase before going to Maryland. I could not wait to hang out with Justin in Maryland for Valentine's Day. While driving to Maryland, I could not believe I made it out of my mother's dungeon. I felt like I just jumped on the freedom express train. I called my job while on the way to Maryland. I told my supervisor I would not be returning to work due to a family situation. Nancy told me if I ever wanted to return to call her, and I could have my job back. Though I agreed, I had no plans of going back. One hour into our drive, Justin's father, Mr. Gills, called Justin to complain that Lehigh had called him saying I had left my mother's residence. Mr. Gills requested that I call my mother and Lehigh. I agreed to call once I arrived in Maryland. Justin and I laughed as we made jokes about my mother and Lehigh's face when they noticed I had moved.

I called my mother as soon as I arrived at Justin's sister's house. My mother could not wait to tell me how she was disappointed with me for leaving her house. I could hear Lehigh in the background, saying, "You ain't right, you know what you did ain't right." I told my mother I was okay and that I would call her once I arrived back in Virginia before hanging up the phone. Justin and I made jokes and laughed about my getaway for the rest of the night. We hung out all day Saturday for Valentine's Day before Justin drove me back to Virginia on Sunday.

Justin and I arrived at my Aunt's Beth's house. Justin met Aunt Beth and Uncle Scott, who talked to Justin about my move, before he headed back to school in Baltimore. Aunt Beth had a three-bedroom house; I shared a room with my cousin Tina, Aunt Beth and Uncle Glenn shared a room, and Uncle Scott had his own room. I called my father, who had moved out of Aunt Beth's house and married a woman from his church. I told him I was living with Aunt Beth and about the living space. He just said okay, probably hoping I did not ask to come to his house to live. But I made the best of my life situation, I even started calling my mother to check on her, Michael, and Brandy. She would often say, "We are okay" before ending the conversation. She never stayed on the phone with me for over five minutes. Until one day, my mother called me to talk. She told me she was upset with me for leaving her house. She said I was rude and disrespectful. With anger in her voice, she told me, "You wait until you have children, they are going to be to you as you were to me." And though I said nothing, I refused to let the words my mother spoke penetrate my mind. Once she finished expressing herself, I told her I would call her next week to check on her, Brandy, and Michael before ending our conversation.

During my first week of living at Aunt Beth's house, one late night while sleeping, I woke up as I heard a scraping sound coming from my bookbag. I was so scared and had awakened Tina to tell I heard something in my bookbag. She woke up and started laughing as she scratched her head. She said, "Dam maine, you must have food in your bookbag, huh?" I did not respond to her, I was more surprised at her response. She said, "We got mice maine, you can't be leaving no food in your bags and stuff. You gotta keep your food in the fridge, or my tin can over there on the floor." She began laughing as she shook my bookbag once and before I could blink my eyes, the mouse had jumped out of my bag and swiftly ran out of her room through the gap under her door. She continued laughing hysterically, as the expression of disgust spread across my face. She said, "Go to sleep, Ben," (the name of their house mouse) "You gonna be right," and she went back to sleep soon after. I was so scared to close my eyes to go back to sleep. I prayed God would not let me be bitten by the mouse. That was the first time I had seen a mouse, but it would not be my last time seeing one in their house.

Though I had enrolled in school, I found myself more concerned about what Justin was doing, I started missing classes and taking several trips to Baltimore throughout the semester. I started feeling like Justin was attending school and chasing the skirts of attractive girls at the HBCU he attended. I refused to sit on the sideline and wait to find out, so I started talking to a guy named Miguel from my math class, whenever I would go. Miguel was very handsome and, academically, he was intelligent. He lived alone and had a new model Mustang car. He would come to Aunt Beth's house to pick me up, and we would hang out. Once, we went out to dinner, and afterwards to his apartment. As we began watching a movie in his bedroom, he received a visit from his friend Ramon. I listened as Miguel and Ramon started talking loudly in the living room. I went to the bathroom, and when I came out of the bathroom, I glanced to see what Miguel was doing. I saw Miguel counting several stacks of money as if he was a stripper and had just collected his ones off the floor. They started smoking weed. I quickly went back to his room, laying on his bed, thinking, "What the hell am I doing?" Miguel soon came back into his room after Ramon left. I told him I had to leave to go back to Aunt Beth's house since I was trying to stick to my curfew. Miguel agreed and kissed my forehead with the softest lips as if he knew I knew about his lifestyle, and I would not want to see him anymore. We found other things to talk about on my ride home. And, though I wanted to see Miguel again, I did not want to be caught up in any foolishness, remembering my conversation with my patient at the assisted living facility.

After I finished my first semester of school, I received my grades and found out I had failed three of my four classes. I was also placed on academic probation. I had to meet with the college board members to determine if I could register for the following semester. Although I was not surprised, I was more so disappointed in myself. I felt like I had lost my ambition, and I was not sure if I could handle life's obstacles the same way I had before. I felt myself becoming hopeless. I wanted a relationship with my mother and father to navigate through this thing called life. I needed help with positive life decision-making and decisions on obtaining healthy relationships. I soon found out that people could let you down, but God always remained the same.

The day before meeting with the school board members, I called into a live gospel radio station requesting prayer from Pastor Lynwood, who was live on the radio. I informed him that I was on academic probation and that I would be meeting with the board the next day. I asked him to pray for me, that God would grant me His *Favor* and I would be able to continue my studies, and my financial aid would be reinstated. Pastor Lynwood prayed for me and told me that God was going to grant me *Favor* with the school board members. He said, "Don't mess up this time, you got a second chance," with which I agreed after he ended his prayer. Once off the phone, I praised God all through Aunt

Beth's house. I made a promise to God that I would stay focused on all my studies and that I would accomplish my goal of obtaining my Associate Degree.

The next day I attended the meeting with one of the board members, Ms. Brown. She was representing the whole board that day. She asked me a series of questions about the cause of missing several days from my classes, and what I planned to do differently if taken off academic probation. I confidently answered Ms. Brown's questions almost as if I knew she would say, "Okay, you can enroll in new classes tomorrow." I knew what God said, and I believed Him. After thirty minutes of meeting with Ms. Brown, she told me she planned to follow up with me in two weeks via mail. As I got up to thank her and to exit the room, Ms. Brown pointed to my shirt and said, "Just knock it off." Not sure what she was talking about until I looked at my shirt. I was embarrassed to see a big roach crawling on the side of my shirt. I was so embarrassed because I knew it came from home. That brown boy had ridden the bus with me and hung on to me as I walked two blocks to my meeting at school. I did as she said and knocked it to the floor before stomping on it and telling her, "Thank You, and you have a good evening."

After my meeting, I took the bus straight home. Still embarrassed, I told Tina, who was waiting at the kitchen table for my arrival. I told her about the roach on my shirt, hanging on to me until the end of my meeting. As expected, she began laughing, falling out of the kitchen chair. Though I was disgusted, I then started laughing too. Despite my laughing along, I thought to myself there was no way I could get use to this type of living with creatures of all kinds. Tina and I were each other's comfort, Aunt Beth and Uncle Scott often worked, leaving Tina in the house alone until one of them would arrive home. Now that I was staying at Aunt Beth's, I was home with Tina. We would always laugh about everything, especially at night when everyone had already gone to bed. We would recall events that happened during our day and just laugh about the oddest things that happened. Aunt Beth would say, "Ay, go to bed. Y'all doing all that damn laughing in there. We trying to get some sleep." Though she was mad, this was something else we would laugh at before falling asleep. Tina and I would do the silliest things like wait for Uncle Glenn to come home and hide in his room until he shut his room door to scare him. He would say, "Got damn, y'all stop playing all the damn time," before he began cursing and slamming his door. One time, Uncle Glenn had purchased a car, an '89 Mercury Cougar. He was so proud of his car he came home showing it off to Uncle Scott, Tina, and me before letting me drive it to Seven Eleven to purchase some snacks. Even though I knew how to drive and a little about cars, I could not figure out the cause of the burning smell coming from Uncle Glenn's car. Tina and I quickly made our purchase before arriving home to Uncle Glenn and Uncle Scott, who were still standing in the same position on the lawn. Before I could get out of the car, Uncle Glenn raced over to the car opening the door complaining about the smell. I quickly gave him his car key and ran back into the house. Tina and I ran up the steps, not wanting to hear his complaints. It was then, I realized I did not lift the lever to release the brake before driving his car. I heard him come into the house and say, "Ay Joi' where you at? You left my damn brake on! Why...." When he finished cursing at me, he left the house. Tina and I laughed so hard, dropping our chips on the floor as we fell on the bed. We both knew before night fell, we had to get the chips up off the floor before the house mouse Ben, and his brothers came to visit us.

Two weeks after attending the meeting with Ms. Brown at the Community College, I received a letter in the mail from Ms. Brown. The letter stated I was approved to enroll into classes for the Fall semester. I praised God all over again, thanking Him for a second chance. I quickly completed my financial aid application before registering for the Fall semester. I changed my major from Nursing to Community and Social Services. I started a new job at the local department store at the mall. I was on my way to a new beginning. I had made two friends named Mercy and Grace. They both were from Kenya. They were nice girls and very genuine. We worked at the department store together. They also attended J. Sargeant Reynolds Community College. We would take the bus together to work some days and take our lunch break at the same time. Though at times, I could barely understand what they were saying, I would often just laugh with them and shake my head as if I understood them. We worked together until the spring semester started. Then, our schedules changed, and we would soon drift apart. I would never forget them or their names, for their names were my constant reminder of God's Mercy and His Grace that always kept me.

On Sunday mornings, Aunt Beth, Tina, cousin Lewis (Aunt Beth' son), and I started attending a church in the city. The church was like my best friend Lia's church from my youth, except the women in the church did not have dollies on their heads. Everyone dressed in their beautiful church attire. All the women only wore skirts and dresses. I sat and watched as Pastor James began talking about the goodness of God, and how He would turn your life around if you would just trust Him. Pastor James turned in my direction and said, "Many are the afflictions of the righteous, but the Lord delivereth him out of them all." (Psalm 34:19). The young man on the organ began playing, and the drummer started drumming. One by one, people popped up like popcorn, dancing and running around the church. I sat in church, looking around, too mature to laugh. I was more so curious, wanting to know more about God on another level. Tina and I would come home after church on Sundays, trying to dance like the people in the church. We would jokingly sing songs the choir members had sung, adding a little vibrato giving the song some exaggeration. Every night we began praying together for we both wanted more of God.

I remember once going to the church's Holy Convocation on a Wednesday night. Tina and I sat in the back section of the auditorium during service. After the praise team had sung, the guest Pastor asked everyone to start thanking God for His presence. He said, "For in the presence of the Lord there is fullness of joy." A few minutes later, the auditorium was full of worship. It was a group sound I had never heard before. The sound and the atmosphere in the auditorium was simply amazing to witness. The Pastor preached out of the Bible, followed by a request that everyone begin praising God for what he was about to do in our lives. I instantly stood up and then Tina stood up as well before giving praises to God. I started thinking of things I needed God to do in my life and my family's life, and I began praising God as the man started playing the organ and the drummer began playing the drums. I remember standing up and praising God. Suddenly, the spirit of God had come upon me. I began jumping up and down and moving my arms and legs as if I had a fire within me. Tina was trying to help me by holding me, so I didn't fall. This experience happened so fast and, once it was over, I just began to cry. In my mind, I was wondering what had just happened. That day I was reminded that the presence and the power of God was real.

On Sundays, I could not wait to attend church. Aunt Beth, Tina, cousin Lewis, and I would attend church faithfully every Sunday. We would listen to the sounds of John P. Kee and Fred Hammond as we sang along to every song while getting dressed for church. I enjoyed hearing the Word of God, preached by Pastor James. Some Sundays, it was like he had listened to my conversations throughout the week. He would preach about the same things I had talked about to my friends. After I joined the church, I soon understood the scripture, "So then faith cometh by hearing, and hearing by the word of God." I never missed a Sunday at church. My relationship with God was strong. It was like I had a fire I never knew I had. I would always invite my friends to church, always telling them about the goodness of God and I prayed for them as they would confide in me about their life's struggles and concerns.

One time my friend, Jamie, and I went to a popular spot in Richmond called Shockoe Bottom. While people were having dinner, drinking, and hanging out; we began witnessing to three young men, one of which I went to middle school with, about Jesus Christ. We told our testimony of the ways God had moved in our lives and gave them an invitation to our church. We held their hands and prayed for them after our twenty-minute encounter. They thanked Jamie and me before walking away. I would often meet people on the bus on the way to school and invite them to my church. I was excited about God. I began talking to

God as if He was standing right next to me. I talked to God about everything that was on my mind like He was one of my best friends and comforter, we had that type of relationship.

I only had one long black skirt that I wore to church which I purchased from Express. I often wore my skirt almost every other Sunday, switching up my shirts to match my black skirt to make a new outfit. I did not have many church clothes, I made the best with what I had. After a few months of attending church, I began to witness the downfalls of church people. It seemed like I did not fit in with the other young women in the church. They just looked at me and judged me by my appearance. I saw the cliques in the church; and, if you did not look or act like them, you were not invited in. I thought, not in the church too. I felt like I was in school all over again. I often thought this was not supposed to happen in the church. Outside of the church, yes, but not inside the church too. One Sunday, Sister Paula (Pastor James' nurse) came to me after church service. She said, "Hey Sister Joi' look at you, you always wearing them same 'ol clothes to church, that same skirt and black tights. Do you not have anything else better to wear to church?" She smiled, waiting for a response. I walked away thinking, *'If I did not know God, this would be my last Sunday I attended church.'* I made up in my mind after all I had been through in my twenty years that I had come too far to turn back now. Sister Paula had issues of her own anyway, so I couldn't let Sister Paula, or the other young women distract me from attending church. This was the church I received my spiritual nourishment from. This was the church that increased my Faith through the Word of God, preached by Pastor James. This was the church that I often received a personal word from Pastor James, who Prophesied to me as he was led by God.

I remember going to Howard University homecoming in the year 1999 with Tee, my only friend from church. Tee was very adventurous. She liked going to places in and out of the state and did not care if she went alone. She was a "get up and go" type of person. I believe if she had a plane, she would travel the world in a week by herself. We talked and laughed about events in our lives that we had experienced during our ride to the homecoming. I always picked and chose what I wanted people to know about me. I felt everyone was not worthy to hear my story. I had always been this way. As a child, I made a vow to myself to never look like what I was going through and never tell people about it. When Tee and I arrived at Howard University, there were crowds of people talking and dancing in the streets. There were so many beautiful young black people. I thought maybe I should have come to DC. It reminded me of high school, but unlike the high school I had graduated from in Maryland. We mingled with the crowd, talking to different people from different zip codes who talked about everything but Jesus. I met a young man from Chicago named Clay, who I would continue to talk to throughout the years. He was very intriguing. He stood out from the rest, looking like he just left the college prep academy.

We talked for hours as if it were just me and him. Tee stood on the sideline, watching, and waiting for me to take a break from our conversation. Before long, she interrupted our conversation. She said, "Joi', I'm hungry, and we gotta go. It's late, and we have to go to church in the morning." Clay and I exchanged phone numbers and planned to talk every day. Although I was still in my long-distance relationship with Justin, I was not sure how much longer it would last. I had not seen him in over a month and was unsure of what he was doing with his free time. After our time mingling at the homecoming, Tee drove back to Richmond while I recapped bits of my conversation with Clay. Tee talked about her observations of homecoming as well, while I listened and smiled, thinking about Clay. I fell asleep during the drive home, but suddenly I had awakened and looked over at Tee who was falling asleep while driving. I quickly called her name to tell her she was falling asleep, and I would continue the drive home. As she pulled over for me to continue the drive home, I thanked God in my head. I thought to myself, I couldn't die. I had a bright future ahead of me, and I wanted to have more conversations with Clay.

After several months of faithfully attending church Sunday service, Bible Study, and singing in the choir, my relationship with God had started becoming more in-depth.

I was praying throughout my day more and believing God by Faith for things I would have never thought to believe Him for. I prayed for my mother and even started praying for Lehigh faithfully. I started working at one of the major banks in the city. After working for six months, I had applied for an apartment. My friends told me I would need a co-signer, so I called my father to tell him I needed a co-signer for an apartment. Before I could finish my sentence, he interrupted me, "Look here, that's your apartment, and if you want it Joi' you have to get it on your own." For some reason, I was surprised by his response. I thought my father would be happy for me and willing to help, or at least that was what I wanted to happen. My father had been very supportive over the past four years. He paid for my driving courses in high school, provided me with money if I asked for it, and often provided me with guidance concerning God. He even gave me my first Bible. I refused to ask my mother because I believed I would receive the same response. I prayed to God and asked for His Favor with the leasing agent. I had no credit, just Faith. I believed God by Faith that He would work it out for me, and I would be able to get the apartment on my own. After several days of waiting, I called the apartment leasing manager to check on the status of my application. I was placed on hold for a few minutes before the leasing manager informed me my application was approved. I praised God, dancing in the middle of the floor of Aunt Beth's living room. I was twenty years old and, for the first time, I had a place of my own to live. A place I could laugh as loud as I wanted, pray if I wanted, and dance on the living room floor if I wanted. I had a place I could finally call *my home.*

OBEDIENCE

" ....Behold, to obey is better than sacrifice "
1 Samuel 15:22

───────────◇───────────

In the Spring of 2000, I moved into my first one-bedroom apartment. My mother and Lehigh had given me bedroom furniture and purchased a mattress and box spring. My father gave me a television and a stand to put in my living room. My Godmother purchased towels and sheets while I bought food and cheap pots and pans. Once everyone left, I closed my door and danced in the middle of my floor like I had lost my mind. I continued to believe God for everything. If my money was low and I needed food, I would leave my cabinets open and pray to God for an increase. Once God sent my cousin Lisa to my apartment to bring me twenty dollars. I say God sent her, because I had not seen her in years and for her to bring me a well needed twenty dollars, I knew only God sent her. As soon as she left, I quickly went to the store and purchased chicken and vegetables. Some nights, I would lay prostrate before God in prayer without having a thought of a roach or a mouse crawling on me. I called on God for everything. He always heard my cry and came to see about me. Managing responsibilities were already instilled in me. I would wake up every morning by 5:30am to shower, get prepared for my day, and make a sandwich to eat while I walked across a huge field at the Veterans hospital to take the bus to work. I would often talk to God as if He was walking next to me while I walked. I had such a peace I forgot about the long walk I had to endure to catch the bus. I would follow up on my conversation with God on the bus as I prayed in my mind, often listening for His voice. After work at 4:30pm, I would take the bus to class and then another bus from class back home. I arrived home every night at 9:30pm, with just enough time to shower, eat, and study before going to bed. This had become my routine five days a week in the rain, sleet, and snow for eight months. I would pray each morning and night that my angels would go before me and protect me. I also would pray that no weapon formed against me would prosper every morning before leaving my apartment. Living in the city, something was always happening, and some people saw no real value in other people's lives, so I had to gird myself in prayer.

Despite moving out of Aunt Beth's house, I was still attending church when I could catch a ride with Tee. Attending church, work, and school had become my new lifestyle. I did not have time to do much of anything outside of these activities. Justin drove down to visit me a few times, but I soon ended our long-distance relationship. Tina once told me that while Aunt Beth visited Pastor James to talk about her life challenges and concerns, he told her that Justin was destroying me. Although Justin and I were in two different states, we still tried to hang on to our fading relationship. However, the mind games, manipulation, and uncertainty was starting to take a toll on me. This was the confirmation I needed, I decided to end my relationship with Justin to focus on my relationship with God, my studies, and on work to keep my apartment. Justin and I remained friends, we talked on the phone occasionally. I even distanced myself from Clay. He was far away in Chicago. Though we spoke weekly, making plans to visit each other, I did not see it happening. After my relationship with Justin ended, that following weekend Tee and Tina spent the night at my apartment for my comfort. Tee argued with me, up and down, that her car was legally parked in a tenant's parking lot when I told her she had to move her car. As night fell, Tina and I were hungry and wanted a Wendy's chicken sandwich and french fries. However, Tee did not want to drive. Later that night, as we were going to sleep, I heard a sound of something rattling, almost like the sound of the mouse that was in my bookbag at Aunt Beth's house. I jumped up and cut the light on only to find Tee secretly trying to open a candy bar. Tina and I looked at each other and laughed as if we were thinking the same thing, "BEN" the mouse. We made Tee share her candy bar with us, since we were still hungry. So, Tee agreed to take Tina and me to Wendy's but after getting dressed, we went outside to find that Tee's car was gone. It had been towed. Tee was mad, I could see the smoke coming out of her nostrils and ears. I thought, 'Girl, you should have listened to me,' but sometimes you can't tell people about what they think they know. Tina and I were so hungry, but we still managed to laugh, rolling on my bare living room floor while Tee stood outside to call the towing company.

My Godmother called me one evening after I came home from school. She told me she had purchased me a manual 1983 Honda Accord for five hundred bucks. She said that I would have to make installment payments to pay her back and I quickly agreed. After ending our conversation, I was so happy I danced all through my 650 square foot apartment, thanking and praising God. The next Saturday, my Godmother had taken me to view and pick up the car she had found in a newspaper ad. Though the car was sixteen years old, it was like a brand-new car straight off the lot. I called cousin Lewis at home, to tell him the good news. Before the end of the night, he taught me how to drive my car. Fred Hammond's "Purpose by Design" was the one tape I played faithfully in my car. I loved Fred Hammond. Without reading my Bible, Fred allowed me to know that I was Blessed. The lyrics were so inspiring, "I was Blessed in the city, and Blessed in the field, Blessed when I came in and Blessed when I went out." I was so full of being Blessed when people asked me how I was doing, I would just say, "I'm Blessed." I thought, if I could ever meet Fred Hammond, I would just say two words to him, "Thank You." His music ministry had brought me through so many situations. As I listened to "Jesus Be A Fence," I got so excited. I could now drive to church, school, work, the mall, and the grocery store. I no longer had to walk and wear out my shoes. God had outdone Himself for me. I received a car, had been attending school, and had even accepted a new position at the main branch of the bank. I would often pick up Brandy and Michael for the weekend. We went to the movies, out to eat, to the mall, and church on Sunday.

One Sunday at church, Pastor James gave an altar call for those who wanted to accept Jesus Christ in their lives. My eyes were closed during the altar call and, afterward, he asked those that had raised their hand to come to the altar. Michael, at the age of seven, had slid past me as we stood on the fourth row of the church. He went to the altar to give his young life to Jesus Christ. Michael never said much about his mother, but I always reminded him that his smile was just like hers. This was the smile he displayed at the altar as Pastor James prayed over him.

Working as a bank teller at the main branch downtown, I met so many friendly people with plenty of money. I even met some people with no money who just wanted to come into the bank to make conversation. I always told them about Jesus and invited them to my church. I was single, and I was not entertaining any Satan-sent distractions. At the bank, I had the task of providing excellent customer service, opening accounts, and telling customers about the bank's new products, and services. I provided excellent customer service, but I refused to be the super jolly bank teller. I made sure to be my professional self and always smile through the challenges that came with my position. I was only three days away from my one-year evaluation, and every day I reminded my Supervisor Debbie, when I walked past her office. I expected a pay increase. On the day of my evaluation, I met with Debbie. She spoke to me about the feedback she received from her Supervisor Janice, regarding my job performance. I listened with no objection as Debbie discussed that my customer service skills were weak, my facial expressions were unfriendly, and my drawer was once short three dollars and eighteen cents. Disappointed, I stared at her trying to remain professional. Debbie then summed up my overall job performance as being fair. In her conclusion, she said, "We have decided to place you on probation for six months." Debbie and I created strategies that I should follow to improve my job performance. Knowing that I was prompt to work every day, never called out sick, opened several checking and saving accounts as required, and provided excellent customer service. I did something that I never thought I would ever do. I built up the courage to type up a resignation letter when I returned to my teller station. I sealed it in a bank envelope and handed it to Debbie. I thought, when you know God, you know He will provide. I put my Faith and trust in God knowing that if He Blessed me with this job, He would Bless me with another job. I had cashed out my 401k and pinched off that money for three months. I was out of work for those three months. My electricity was never shut off, my bills were paid, and my rent was never late.

During the three months I was not working, I took a well-needed trip to Delaware to visit my friend, Natasha. She had moved into an apartment close to the University of Delaware. We attended one of her friend's parties and had a lot of fun hanging out in the downtown area. While at Natasha's apartment, I called Carl, who had still not forgotten about the time I stood him up. We talked for about thirty minutes, before he told me that he was coming in one hour to visit me at Natasha's house. However, he never did. Natasha and I laughed so much that night, making jokes about Carl still being mad. We also had time to catch up on each other's life changes. While hanging out with Natasha, I started to feel like I wanted to move to Delaware. I wanted a break from life's responsibilities. My life was tough. Everything I had, I had to work hard for it and hard to keep it. I hardly went to any parties or had time to hang out, like in high school. Although I did go to a couple of parties once I moved back to Virginia, the parties in Virginia were dangerous to attend. I remember going to one party where there was a big commotion. I was dancing to Camp Lo's "Luchini," and I heard firecrackers. I thought, 'This party is hype. They are drinking and got firecrackers going off.' Until my friend Kim said, "Girl, you better get down 'dey shooting in here." As I kneeled, I noticed I was the only one still standing up. Unlike the parties I was used to in high school, everybody just wanted to dance, drink alcohol, and get as many numbers as they could. I felt like I was missing out on life. I mainly went to church, school, and work. I discussed with Natasha about moving in with her, to which she agreed. Natasha and I talked about how we could become roommates to save money while obtaining our goals. I planned to find employment and transfer to a college in Delaware, it was the perfect plan.

Once I returned home, I called the church office leaving a voice message for Pastor James. I informed him that I was moving to Delaware in one month. I wrote a letter to my leasing company informing them of the date I planned to move out of my apartment, and that I had no plans to renew my lease. I was so excited about my plans to move that I had started packing up items in my apartment. I planned to give away some items and to take some with me to Delaware. The next Sunday, I went to church as usual. The praise team sang songs that caused praise to break out in the church. John played the life out of the organ, and Sam broke one of his sticks playing on the drums. I joined in with the members of the church who shouted and danced like never before. I danced in the middle of the floor. I danced over my disappointments, loneliness, and pain that I was still quietly experiencing. I was also praising God for my new beginning in Delaware. As I opened my eyes and took my seat. Pastor James soon took the mic and began talking about the goodness of God before informing the congregation of his sermon topic. He said, "Look at your neighbor and tell them the topic of today's message, which is titled, Moving Outside the Will of God." The more I sat listening to the message, the more I wanted to get up and go home. I began rocking my leg, thinking '*I know he ain't preaching about me.*' Although I knew God was speaking directly to me, I was so devastated because I was moving to Delaware in one month. Pastor James began talking about the saints running when things get too hard and too tough. He said, "Some fires you have to sit in, for there was character and substance God was building and putting in his chosen people." After anxiously waiting for his message to end, he finally concluded his message with, "Behold, to obey is better than sacrifice." Once the church service was over, I walked so fast out of church, I did not say anything to anybody. I couldn't wait to get to my car to have a conversation with God. I told Him, "I was mad because I gave up my apartment, and now, I had to stay in Virginia when I wanted to go to Delaware." I was twenty-one, and I had no life of fun. I wanted to date, party, and hang out as I did in high school. I wanted fewer responsibilities. After I ended my pity party, with tears running down my cheeks, I told God I would be obedient. I knew His will for my life was better than my will. After crying for what seemed to be a few hours, I had gotten my voice together to call Natasha and tell her I would not be moving to Delaware. As if she knew the phone call was coming, she just said, "Okay" without asking any questions. I called my Godmother to determine if I could live with her, without her asking I explained why I was moving out of my apartment. Though she said yes, I knew I would miss living on my own.

One afternoon I went to my mother's house for comfort, as I arrived in the driveway, I saw Grandma sitting on the front porch in a wheelchair staring at the sky. She looked frail in stature, her legs were crossed as if they were stuck together, she even looked like she had shrunk several inches. I hugged and kissed her without mentioning her appearance. I was glad to see Grandma. She didn't say much, she just shook her head up and down for "yes" and sideways for "no," when I asked her a million questions. My mother met me on the porch to tell me Grandma was diagnosed with diabetes and she had developed a sore on her leg that gangrene had set in. My mother had scheduled medical services for Grandma since her doctor in North Carolina reported he could not treat the gangrene. My mother said Grandma was staying at her house for the past two weeks. She discussed planning to drive her back to North Carolina after her treatment was completed. It was at that moment, Grandma said, "That's if I want to go back!" I laughed so hard because I did not think she could talk with her, mostly nonverbal responses. I made sure to visit Grandma almost every day after class. Visiting her took my mind off my problems. The day Grandma left to go back to North Carolina, I told her I would visit her soon and call to check on her. She gave me a hug and kiss as my mother helped her into the car.

Within three months, I began working with elementary school children with behavior challenges at an alternative school. All the students were expelled from public school and placed in the alternative school. Most of the students were diagnosed with Oppositional Defiant Disorder, Attention Deficit Disorder, or Attention Deficit Hyperactivity Disorder. This was a new field in which I had no previous experience. I was not even sure I was qualified for the position. I learned de-escalation skills, restraint techniques, and crisis intervention skills. After one week of training, I was already exhausted. I was assigned to work one on one with a six-year-old boy named Ralph, who was diagnosed with Attention Deficit Hyperactivity Disorder. Ralph was very repetitive. He would ask the same question fifteen times and would receive the same answer each time. During my first week working with Ralph, I sat next to him as his teacher discussed his assignments for the day. Ralph began asking the same question. He kept asking, "Can you take me outside to play?" He continued to ask, despite me telling him about five times, "Ralph, after you complete your assignment, then I will take you outside." After the sixth time, he asked again, I did not answer, I responded with silence. He then looked at me as I sat next to him and yelled, "Fuck you den, bitch. I want to go outside." I just sat in my chair, shocked. I remember thinking did this little boy just cuss at me. Though

I remained professional knowing that Ralph attended the alternative school for a reason, I calmly told him, "Ralph, I will take you outside to play once you finish your assignment." To my surprise, in a soft tone, he responded by saying, "Okay." This behavior continued for six months until I was assigned a new student named Steven, who was in the same classroom as Ralph. Ralph was assigned to a new Counselor to work with for the rest of the school year.

Steven was eight years old. One day he got upset with the teacher and threw a pencil at him. When I addressed him, he charged at me, trying to grab my neck. I quickly grabbed his hands. He then started kicking me. Steven was physically aggressive and verbally aggressive in comparison to Ralph, who was verbally aggressive. I held his hands and started the physical restraint process. He said, "You can't handle me, bitch," as he bit my hand. Though his bite was very painful, I managed to restrain Steven alone. I held him until my coworker came to relieve me. My supervisor told me to go to the company's clinic. She said, "This happens all the time, you just have to receive a tetanus shot and a three series test due to a possible body fluid exchange." Though this was an intense position, I maintained my position for three years before leaving the company.

In my last case, as a One on One Counselor, I was at another alternative school. This school looked like a house with small classrooms instead of bedrooms. All the students and staff seemed like a big family. There were about forty students in the school. I was assigned to work with a student named Kelly, who was the brother of Steven. I made sure to wear dress pants with sneakers just in case he was like his brother and had to be restrained. While working with Kelly, I met Thomas, one of the male staff members at the small school. He was very tall, very funny, and attractive. He always talked about getting married. Though I was not interested in marriage after a few months, we began hanging out. I started talking to him about God and why we needed to live for Him. I invited him to church, and one day he attended. He even participated in the New Year fifteen days of Fasting and Praying which Pastor James had instructed for the congregation. After the consecration, we went to Tysons Corner Center to shop. We even took pictures at the huge mall and since it was Valentine's Day, he brought me several unexpected gifts. He started staying overnight at my Godmother's house, with whom I had moved in. My Godmother soon noticed my glow. She said, "You and Thomas getting real friendly aren't y'all? 'Cause I'm tired of seeing him sleeping on my couch." Although she was right, I just laughed as I left out the door to meet Thomas, who was waiting outside for me.

We were headed to his friend Larry's house for dinner. Once we arrived at Larry's house, I felt like I was in an interview. Larry and his soon to be wife Kim asked me questions about my goals, my major in school, and how Thomas and I met. Though I struggled with some of my "interview" answers, Thomas was right there to coach me along. I could tell by the look on their faces that they were not impressed and did not think Thomas and I would not last long. A month later, I saw the happy couple again at a wedding that Thomas and I attended for their mutual friend William. Larry just smiled while Kim waved, probably thinking, "Thomas and Joi' still hanging on." Thomas was consuming my time with hang outs and overnight stays at my Godmother's house. Thomas was seven years older than me; he seemed mature, yet fun to be around. However, Thomas began asking to have sex with me which was something I was not willing to do, so I began to pull away from him. I gave him back all the Valentine's Day gifts he bought me and the pictures we took together. However, Thomas insisted I keep them. This was my last semester in school anyway, and I decided I needed to stay focused on school. When I saw him at work, I would talk to him about God. I tried to keep my focus on Kelly, my student, since he was my main reason for working at the school.

Anthony, another friend at work, noticed Thomas' intentions and told me to be careful with Thomas. Anthony seemed as if he was trying to protect me. He would find ways to make conversation, just as Thomas would come and talk to me. Soon, Anthony and I started hanging out. We would share our relationship concerns and often talked about God and our future goals. Anthony was one year older than me. He was in the process of earning his master's degree in

Political Science at the local University. His thought process was way advanced than the average person my age or even older. Though this angel of a man was trying to steer me in the right direction, away from Thomas, I couldn't stop thinking of all the fun Thomas and I had. Thinking I had everything under control, I started back with Thomas again. Thomas played on my heartstrings for a month. And when he was unable to get what he wanted, he distanced himself from me. He had stopped accepting my phone calls and after one month, it was like he had stopped coming to work. After my assignment was completed with Kelly, the thought of seeing Thomas was no more. The heartbreak was a struggle for me because I knew I should have listened to my intuition. I also received a warning from Anthony, who turned out to be right about Thomas. I was heartbroken and hurt because I was in too deep. I had to pull myself together since I would be graduating in two months. One day I had to look in the mirror and tell myself, "Get yourself together, girl. You are about to graduate in two months. You have no time to cry over someone that was not meant for you." This was my first heartbreak, not knowing that it would not be my last with him.

Two weeks before my graduation, I invited my family members to attend. My mother informed me that she was not sure if she, Brandy, and Michael would attend. She never really gave a reason why and I did not ask. My father told me he had to attend his church service on the day of my graduation. He was a Seven Day Adventist, and he observed the Sabbath day on Saturday. Though I was disappointed and hurt all over again, I was well over age and had to get over my feelings. Afterall, I was about to graduate. I had made it through school. Despite being on and off academic probation, not being able to move to Delaware, having struggles in my personal and family relationships. I had accomplished my goal. As my name was called, I heard cousin Lewis, Tamora, and Yonce yelling my name and clapping, while my Godmother and my friends began shouting and cheering as I walked across the stage. I had the biggest smile, and I felt so proud of myself. If I had not been obedient and stayed in Virginia, who knows if I would have ever graduated from college. And, though I was still heartbroken about Thomas, the feeling on that day, was priceless.

BREAKTHROUGH

"O give thanks unto the Lord; for he is good:
because his mercy endureth for ever."
Psalm 118:1

———————◇———————

One Sunday, while driving home after church, I
received a phone call from Thomas. In a calm
voice, he said, "Hey, I was just calling to check up
on you. How have you been? You alright?" I had to look at
my phone twice to see if this was the phone number of the
Thomas that had broken my heart. I quickly stated, "I'm
well, I just left a church service." He told me about his status,
as if I had asked. Through this one conversation of Thomas
checking up on me, it opened a door for many more. After a
few conversations, I started staying overnight at Thomas's
house. One late night visit turned into another late-night
visit, then another. Instantly I was emotionally back where I
left off with Thomas, and the previous heartache soon
disappeared. With little effort, Thomas had finessed his way
back into the lonely spot in my heart. One morning, I was
getting ready to leave Thomas' house when I noticed a
woman's undergarment on the side of his bed. Though I did
not say anything to Thomas, I knew I had to leave him alone
for good this time. I began pulling back from Thomas once

again. However, after one missed period and a positive pregnancy test, I knew my life was about to change. I could not believe I was pregnant. The thought of being pregnant at the age of twenty-two was so devastating for me. I knew I should have never let Thomas back into my heart. I thought to myself, 'Why didn't I see this distraction coming?' I felt like I disappointed God. I was maintaining my relationship with God through daily prayer. I was attending church and singing in the choir faithfully, I was even the choir secretary. Now I was pregnant.

I remember telling my Godmother about my pregnancy. She just laughed, saying, "I can't see you being a mother yet, not you." After her response, I did not want to tell anyone else. A few days later, I called Thomas to tell him I was pregnant. He answered the phone as if he knew the reason for my phone call. After telling Thomas I was pregnant, he was silent for at least thirty seconds and finally he said, "Maine, this is a conspiracy." 'A conspiracy?' I thought. As much as I wanted to jump through the phone and head butt him while cursing him out, I couldn't. I just said, "You having sex with me was not a conspiracy it was a choice by you and me," and I calmly hung up the phone. My feelings were so hurt. I had gotten my emotions and mind entangled with Thomas again. I was disappointed in myself and embarrassed I did not have enough self-control to protect myself. I tried to carry on and conduct my days, as usual, trying to block being pregnant and Thomas' response out of my mind. I remember one morning looking at myself in the mirror, saying, "Girl, get yourself together. This is the last day of this. It happened and it is over. You must and you will move on from this." It was like my soul was speaking through me with great conviction.

One day while I was home, I went to the bathroom. After using the bathroom, there was an object at the bottom of the toilet. It had no real color and no real form. I could not make out what the object was. I quickly called my Godmother into the restroom. She informed me that I had miscarried, and the object at the bottom of the toilet was the embryo. At that moment, I felt so many different emotions. I felt sadness, gladness, relief, and a thought that this was a second chance. I called to inform Thomas of the change in my pregnancy status, which he seemed neither glad nor sad. He seemed surprised, quickly asking how it happened. "What happened?" I told him there was no need to worry before hanging up the phone. Still trying to grasp everything that happened and my existing feelings for Thomas, I remembered my mirror talk and telling myself I had to move on.

I began watching the TBN network for hours to take my mind off the miscarriage and Thomas' response. As I listened to the guest Pastors preach about different stories in the Bible, I began applying the Word of God to my current situation. Sometimes the message did not pertain to my situation. But I found a word in the message and made it fit my situation to find encouragement and to draw strength to get through my difficult time.

A few weeks later, by coincidence, I saw Thomas' sister, Kia, at the library. I had no intention of talking about Thomas or the miscarriage, however Kia did. She informed me that Thomas was getting married in a few months. My heart felt like it stopped beating for a few seconds. I just smiled and stayed positive, trying to show little to no emotion. Kia told me about Thomas' fiancé before concluding our conversation, saying, "I wish Thomas would have stayed with you." I just smiled and said, "Well, he knew who he wanted to be with." Kia and I hugged each other before leaving. It was like we would never see each other again. As I walked away, I thought 'Damn, can I get a break?' My heart was going through the healing process. It was difficult to cope with life especially since I had just had a miscarriage, and now to hear Thomas was getting married; it was too much. It was like I had been hit with another blow straight to the face. I had heard of depression but never experienced it before until this experience. I thought, *'How could this happen to me?'*

One evening while I was driving home, Aunt Rose, whom I had not spoken to in months, called to invite me to Bermuda with her and her mother, Mrs. Cheryl. In need of a quick getaway, I gladly accepted her invitation. Two days later, I was on a plane headed to Bermuda. I had plenty of quiet time to reflect and think about my life while on the plane. The thought of Thomas began to fill my mind. I quickly began to pray to God, asking Him to help me move on from the place I was in. I discussed my current life challenges and concerns as if God didn't already know. I asked God to change my direction and to show me His direction for my life. I was talking to God like He was sitting on the other side of the window with His ear to the plexiglass listening to every word. Luckily, I had a window seat, and no one was sitting next to me on the plane. If there was, my seat neighbor would have thought something was wrong. But I needed God to help me. I believed God used Aunt Rose to invite me to Bermuda so that I could sincerely connect with God from my hurt place. As I stared out the window, at one point seeing nothing but white clouds, I felt myself suffocating. Although I was praying to God, it would have been nice to see a piece of the blue sky. I was surrounded by the same white clouds that filled the air. I refused to close my eyes to sleep, for I needed God. Once we got close to our destination, I could see clearly the long stretch of water that surrounded the beautiful island that I could not wait to explore. As I stared out the window, I saw beautiful bright colored homes, tall palm trees, and winding roads. I began reflecting on the scripture in the Bible that read, "The earth is the Lord's and the fulness thereof; the world, and they that dwell therein. For he hath founded it upon the seas and established it upon the floods." (Psalm 24). Knowing if God created the water, the land, and trees which are not flesh, why should I think God could not change me and make me over again for His Glory and grant me what I am requesting. He owns and made it at all. I knew then that I must submit myself totally to Him while watching and praying.

Once on the island, Aunt Rose, Mrs. Cheryl, and I stayed in a beautiful villa with a spacious kitchen and bedrooms. Every morning the sun woke us up, kissing us with its brightness, it was like Heaven to see the crisp blue sky as we opened our eyes. I would walk out to the porch that overlooked the front lawn, which included tall palm trees and other fine greenery. The smell of nature filled the air. I heard the birds chirping so clear as I sat on the chair in the middle of the porch soaking up Bermuda's beauty, God's creation. I thanked God for this trip to Bermuda. It was a beautiful place. It was a place where even if you felt down, it would not last long. The sun was there to poke comfort into that down place. The beaches would sing a peaceful song as the water splashed together. It was a rhythm I enjoyed as I laid on the beach. The island was full of life. The air was peaceful and calm. Everyone was very friendly. They greeted us with a smile. Everyone spoke life into our day, for they called it good, good by day and good by night. We toured the island by boat. We had some retail therapy and ate delicious island food. We even met a family from Philadelphia who was planning to relocate to Bermuda. They informed us of places we should visit before leaving Bermuda. We took a bus to travel around the island to see some of its historical sites. The more we toured the island, the more I had thoughts of relocating to Bermuda. Since arriving, I began imagining all the possibilities of peaceful island life as I enjoyed all that I explored.

Within six months after returning from Bermuda, I moved into my apartment. I also started new employment and purchased a car. I was attending church and had maintained a family life with my mother, Lehigh, Michael, and Brandy. Brandy, Michael, and I were hanging out more on the weekends and attending church together on Sundays. My mother and Lehigh had even attended church with us one Sunday. However, they left early because Lehigh's back was hurting. Brandy and I believed he left early because his inner demons were not comfortable in church. I surrounded my space with good feelings and positive thoughts. My mother, Brandy, and Michael were glad to see that I was visiting more often; however, Lehigh often just mumbled, "Hey," when I would display a bright and happy demeanor when I visited. I was trying to find the good in everything. Most of all, I was consistent with God. I thanked God almost every day for turning around what had taken place in my life. I felt good about the changes and choices I was making.

Though God had turned my life around, I was still lonely. I went on a few dates, which was fun, but sometimes scary. It seemed like most of the guys I attracted had trauma or issues from their childhood. This was true with one guy I dated named Mathis. I remembered him from my first apartment complex. He was cool, down to earth, but a tad bit off sometimes. One day I visited Mathis at his house. He was sitting in a chair in his large living room, rolling up weed. He began telling me a story about growing up in Georgia and how he was teased a lot because he was much shorter and lighter than his friends. Mathis had a complex about his height and skin complexion as a result of this. As Mathis discussed his childhood, he became angry and convincing while telling his story. I thought I should have stayed at home. I felt like I was his therapist during his story time. I knew not to ask the questions therapists tend to ask like, "So how did that make you feel?" or "tell me more about that feeling?" He might have gone from zero to ten in point five seconds. I invited Mathis to come to church with me and to my surprise, he agreed.

The following Sunday, I arrived at Mathis' house, and surprisingly he was on time. He was well-groomed and appeared ready to hear the Word of God. During service, Mathis appeared interested in the sermon. However, as time went on and Mathis started looking anxious, he started looking around like someone was talking to him. The church service lasted longer than usual this Sunday. It lasted longer than what I had told Mathis by my prediction. Mathis became so upset when the church service was over. He complained that he missed his football game. I drove fast the whole drive to Mathis' house. I did not want him to flip out on me.

Once we arrived at his residence, Mathis got out of the car, not saying a word, so I quickly drove away. Before I could reach home, Mathis had called me three times. However, I did not answer. He left three voice messages complaining that I made him miss his football game. As I listened to his voice messages, I could hear the anger in his voice and the sound of his hand hitting the wall. It sounded like he had dropped or threw a couple of dishes. At the end of his last message, he said he was coming to my house to see me since I was not accepting his phone calls. Before he could arrive, I called my cousin Sonya to tell her about Mathis behavior after church. She suggested I get a restraining order. Once she arrived at my apartment, I drove to the police station to get a restraining order against Mathis. I thought all I did was take him to church so he could get his life together. Now he had left three crazy-sounding messages on my phone. When Sonya and I arrived at the police station, I informed the police officer of Mathis' name and the situation that occurred. The police officer ran Mathis' name, and an extra-large mugshot of his face showed up on the screen. I was more scared than when I first entered the precinct. I was too afraid to file a restraining order and quickly left the police precinct. After that day, I never spoke to Mathis again. I thought the Angels of the Lord must have arrested him because no harm came near my dwelling, not even another phone call.

And I was just as lucky when I hung out with my friend, Keona, from work at her boyfriend's house. One late summer evening, I witnessed Keona's boyfriend and his friends drinking alcohol and smoking weed. All of a sudden, the tallest one took out a gun from the back of his pants and ran to the back of the house and fired off about eight shots before running back inside the house with Keona and me. I thought, Lord, please don't let me die tonight. Keona and I quickly left the house. That was the last time I hung out with her.

Then there was the time I met this handsome guy who rode the same bus as me, to the mall near my job. He had the smoothest demeanor. Later that week we went to Applebee's and had the coolest conversation about our lives until the conversation took a swerve. He started talking about sexual acts he wanted to perform on me. He started telling me about the past sexual interactions he had with women who lived in the city. He laughed at my facial expressions before continuing his lustful conversation. You would have thought Satan had moved him out of the chair and had sat down in his place. I quickly said, "I got to go to work tomorrow, so I must get ready to leave." I had forgotten that he drove us in his cousin's car. Instead of taking me home, he took me to a dark park, where he wanted to walk around. He assured me that after we walked around the park, he would take me home. As we walked, I noticed that he was walking too slow. He began talking about his life as a rapper. Not interested, I began walking away from him back to the car. He then grabbed my arm and told me not to walk away from him when he was talking to me. Jesus was with me that night because, with the serious look of madness on my face, he started laughing. He said, "Girl, I was just playing with you. Let's go, let me take you home." Once I was home, I vowed never to go out on any more dates with men who rode the bus or with any man that God did not send. I thanked God for my Angels that watched over and protected me from dangers seen and unseen.

After graduating from Community College, I knew I had to continue my education. So, after returning from Bermuda, I went on three college visits. One of the schools was Virginia State University, I was pleased with the level of hospitality I received from the student tour representative who often talked about the culture of the school. I was also impressed with the academic center of my majoring department. I liked how most of the classroom settings were intimate and the perfect room size conducive for learning. I was even more excited when the Admissions Director told me my credits from J. Sargeant Reynolds Community College were transferable to the University. Within two weeks, I received my acceptance letter, and in the Fall, I entered the School of Psychology program. I was proud to attend an HBCU, I was the first person on both sides of my family to attend a four-year college. During my first year at VSU, I met so many beautiful, creative, and intelligent

Black and Brown students, with so many accents and styles from so many different places. I knew for sure, I had to keep my mind on Jesus and my phone in my pocket because the nice-looking brothers were at VSU! However, I had no time to party and made no time to play games. My focus was on graduating and earning my degree in Psychology. Once I earned my degree, I had plans to move to New York City to contract with the Wilhelmina Modeling Agency. I always wanted to model for high fashion designers, and I also had a backup plan of using my degree in the event I was not successful at obtaining a modeling contract with Wilhelmina Modeling Agency. In my first semester, I enrolled in five classes and two laboratory classes. I arrived to class on time, completed each assignment as requested, and stayed in close communication with my professors. I made a few friends in difficult classes so that I could participate in group studies or discussions for upcoming tests and quizzes.

I was excited about attending school. I wanted to be a part of VSU, not just as a student. I started attending track practice to prepare for tryouts for the VSU track team. However, after a few days of experiencing a high level of intense running, I only made it through two practices before knowing track was not for me. After the first day of practice, my legs were so sore and tight. I felt like I had run a high-speed marathon. By the second practice, I knew I was not coming back. Honestly speaking, I did not have time for track. I worked full-time overnight, and I attended school during the day. I had to schedule my sleep times in between. Not to mention church on Sunday, choir practice on Monday, and Bible Study on Tuesday.

Samantha was one of my first friends at VSU. She was from Harlem, NY. Samantha always had a story to tell that made me walk away thinking my life was not as bad as I thought. She was down to earth, and she had no problems expressing her feelings. We often shared our relationship stories and what we planned to do after we graduated. Samantha was a super senior. She had been attending classes at VSU for five years. She only needed two more classes to graduate. When she was not planning for her graduation, she was playing matchmaker. Samantha called herself secretly, hooking me up with Raymond, a junior from Brooklyn. The three of us were in Mrs. Garcia's Spanish II class. Raymond was a charmer, but he always told the corniest jokes and spent the whole semester trying to figure out why he was taking Mrs. Garcia's Spanish II class. I was not at all interested in Raymond. I liked older guys to hang out with, and Raymond was one year younger than me. However, after Mathis, I felt like I needed to have a thorough interview with Raymond before I even thought of hanging out with him. Throughout the semester, Raymond and I eventually hung out twice. We did not have much in common but passing Mrs. Garcia's Spanish II class. Raymond wanted more; however, I did not want to take that path with my classmate, knowing I would have to look at him again in class. I learned my lesson with Thomas. Raymond and I played it cool throughout the semester by talking on the phone some evenings after class. However, after the semester was over, so were we. Lesson learned. Always stick to your intuition about someone you plan to involve yourself with. Samantha swore it was something I did. She always called me picky. After the bad selection of men, I had no choice but to be picky.

Samantha and I went to the VSU Homecoming game together. We made sure we were super cute on that day. Though we ended up being super cute and cold (our attire did not reflect the weather), you couldn't tell us anything. Once at the game, there were so many people and, for some reason, I was super excited. I did not pay attention to the homecoming game, I showed up more so for the scenery until halftime. Samantha and I danced in the stands as we watched the VSU marching band. This was the first homecoming game at VSU I attended since being in Virginia, and I was hyped! Missy Elliott's "Work It" and Sean Paul's "Gimme the Light" were some of the songs that filled the streets. We sang while stopping to dance in the street. We laughed and stayed together as we talked to some of the alumni and other people we met. When I arrived home, my feet and legs hurt so bad. I felt like I went to track practice instead of homecoming.

The closer I came to completing my courses, school started becoming more difficult. It seemed like I had a paper to write or a test to take or a new project every week. At times, I was not sure if I could maintain my classes. I remember having self-talk sessions where I would have to tell myself to press my way through and not to give up. I began listening to Fred Hammond's album "Speak Those Things" every day for strength while praying to God to help me through the semester. Nothing for me ever came easy. Just because I was attending college, nothing had changed. I went to class during the day, and I worked overnights at a group home for teenage girls with babies. I was assigned to monitor, support, and assist the girls who were all under the age of eighteen and their babies as young as newborns. Although these girls were mothers, they were still children mentally. I felt like I had to be a mother, a teacher, and a role model for these girls. The girls were challenging. They had been removed from their parent's homes and now placed in our group home. Some days, I would go to work, and there was one resident that would always try to disobey the rules when I came on shift. Her son would always be in her bed under her blanket while she slept next to him. Luckily, she never rolled on him. I would wake her up to remind her of the house rule not to have her baby in her bed. As soon as she would put him in his crib, he would wake up. She would say, "Miss Joi' can you please take him? I'm tired. I got to go to school in the morning." I would take him, rocking him back to sleep, wishing I could sleep too. Like his mother, I had a class in the morning. If it was not this particular resident asking me to stay up with her child, it would be another. This happened several times throughout the week. After putting the kids to sleep, I would stay up to study or complete papers for school. I worked with the girls and their babies as a Residential Counselor for four years.

One early morning while at work I received a phone call from my mother. She told me Grandma had passed away. Grandma went into a diabetic coma and never woke up. As soon as I heard Grandma passed away, all I could do was think about the conversations I had with her, the lessons she taught me from a child, and how she always wanted to fatten me up when I came to visit her. I cried, thinking about the times I should have picked up the phone to call Grandma or even gone to visit her on my days off.

Two weeks after hearing the news, I drove to New Jersey to attend Grandma's funeral, or should I say family reunion. I saw my cousins, aunts, and uncles I had not seen in several years. Everyone was hugging each other while talking about how much they had changed physically. I could not wait until the funeral was over, just seeing Grandma in the casket made me think of her life and how one minute you can be alive and the next you could be gone permanently. Tears continued to roll down my face as I looked over at my mother and her sisters. Once at the burial site, I noticed Grandma was being buried next to Sharell. I began to think back on when Grandma called me to tell me about Sharell's death. It was at that moment I realized how important my family was despite our differences.

I had one semester left before I graduated from college. During this time, I started dating Josiah, who was like a big kid. He always played video games and made jokes about things the average person would care less about. I met him in the summer of 1997 when I moved back to Virginia. However, we both were in relationships and did not want to cross our friendship line. We soon went our separate ways after hanging out a few times. Five years later, I ran into Josiah at the grocery store. We were both single, so we picked up where we left off. We had several conversations and went on a few dates before spending one night at Josiah's apartment. One night turned into another night. Then I started staying with Josiah every week. Despite having my apartment, I liked staying with Josiah. He was someone who could occupy my lonely time until someone better came along. After three months of seeing Josiah, I became pregnant. All I could think was, 'Not again.' I had one semester left in school before graduating, and Josiah was no one I wanted to have a child with. I remember telling him I was pregnant. He seemed so happy. He probably thought he would have someone with whom to play his video games. Though he was happy, I was not. The result of my last pregnancy continued to play in my mind. Unable to control my emotions, I went to talk to my father, who I thought could hold me together. My father and his wife had divorced, and my father had moved into a two-bedroom apartment. Brandy had moved in with my father after being put out of my mother's house for having a physical fight with Lehigh. I met with my father, who was sitting in his recliner chair, looking as if he was interested in the conversation.

During my visit, I found the perfect opportunity to tell him I was pregnant, or so I thought. I did not waste any time, I got straight to the point, "Dad, I'm pregnant." Brandy had come into the living room and sat down to take a front-row seat at the show that was about to go down. My father gave me this grim stare and said, "I don't know why the hell you are telling me. What do you want me to do?" He cleared his throat before preaching a sermon about my decision making. He brought up my first pregnancy, which I was surprised he knew about. I was unsure who told him and too embarrassed to ask. He discussed how God had given me a second chance, and now I had let Him down again. I listened to my father as he had given me his take on my life. I wanted to cry as my father scorned me with his words. I started flipping through the phone book to find the closest abortion clinic. I was scared and now confused. Then, I quickly thought, 'What am I doing? I couldn't let my father's words cause this type of reaction from me.' I thought I could not kill a child who did not ask to be born because I did not protect myself. How selfish. I also knew God would not be pleased with me, no matter how many times I may have told myself it was okay. With no hesitation, I got up from the wicker chair, which felt like it was about to fall apart and told my father, "I send all your words right back to you," before leaving his apartment. Years later, my father told me that he had a similar experience, he had not been delivered from. He apologized for his tone that day. I guess his anger and rough speech came from this unresolved place while listening to my story.

The next day I scheduled my eight-week prenatal appointment. Although I was six weeks pregnant, I had to wait another two weeks before I could be seen by my doctor. I called Brandy and informed her of my first prenatal visit to see if she could attend the appointment with me since she already knew I was pregnant. The whole ride we talked about the conversation between my father and me. We laughed about some of the things my father said as I drove to my appointment. Even though I was laughing, some of the things my father had spoken were right. But Brandy always kept my spirits high, and I was glad she had come with me to my first appointment.

Once I was seen, I had an ultrasound completed. During the procedure, the nurse quickly ran out of the office, saying she would be right back. When she returned, the doctor returned with her and they reviewed the ultrasound pictures. My doctor turned and looked at me and showed me the fetus had no heartbeat. She told me I had to schedule to have a D&C procedure completed to have the fetus removed from my uterus. I had gotten used to being pregnant, and now knowing that I was no longer pregnant was heartbreaking. Although this time, I did not feel depressed.

I just knew it was a matter of me having this procedure completed. I called Josiah to inform him of my visit to the doctor's office. Josiah showed little emotion. He just said, "It's okay, boo, we have to try again." I looked at my phone in shock at Josiah's response as I hung up. When I arrived at Josiah's apartment, I told him about the procedure and that I needed him to go with me to have the procedure completed. Josiah quickly told me he could not take off work. Without questioning Josiah, I had no choice but to call my mother. I did not tell my mother about the first pregnancy, but I had no choice but to tell her about this pregnancy. I needed her to take me to the hospital to have the procedure completed.

After I told my mother, I could hear the disappointment in her voice. She questioned why Josiah was not going with me to have the procedure completed. I made up a story and told her that he had to go out of town that day. I could hear the disappointment even more in her voice. She informed me that she would attend the procedure with me and that I had to stay at her house until my body had healed. And though she was disappointed in me, I was also disappointed in myself. I was twenty-four years old and had already had two miscarriages. I was not married nor engaged. I often prayed to God, I was still singing in the choir and attending church faithfully. However, I had little control over my flesh. Though I knew God, and I knew what He was able to do, I still struggled with my flesh and controlling my sexual desires. I was able to shake some things through prayer. But this demon seemed like it did not want to release me. I would talk about it with my friends, but they were doing the same thing. So, talking to them was always pointless because we were all in the same situation. Unlike me, they were comfortable and seemed to never get pregnant or have any conviction.

On the day of my procedure, my mother stayed at the hospital throughout the procedure. She had taken off work to accompany me. Once the procedure was completed, I received a Depo Provera shot to prevent any further pregnancies. I made a vow, this was the last time I was going through this. I went to my mother's house to stay for a few days, as she had planned to take care of me. However, later that evening, Josiah arrived at her house and asked me to stay at his house. My mother quickly declined for me; however, I accepted. My mother was devastated. She told us to practice safe sex, and the next time I needed to go to the hospital to call Josiah for any help since he was the one I was having sex with. I was so embarrassed, but I knew what she was saying was good stuff. Josiah, being the big kid that he was, just laughed and said, "Alright, Alright," and began laughing even more. My mother looked at him, and then she turned and looked at me in disgust, shaking her head. She looked as if she was thinking, 'What the hell are you doing with him?' I knew I did not want to stay in a relationship with Josiah, so a few weeks later, I ended our relationship.

Three weeks after receiving the Depo Provera shot, I noticed I was starting to become depressed. It was hard to be normal, I began watching the 4 o'clock news, 5 o'clock news, and 6 o'clock news, which was something I had never done, not realizing the news was causing me to become more depressed. I was unable to focus on school, and I had stopped attending my classes. I had decreased my hours at work to part-time. I just stayed in bed. At times, I thought I saw ants crawling on the wall before looking again and seeing nothing. I called my doctor to inform her of my symptoms, and she said, "Yes, those are some of the symptoms associated with the contraceptive, but you will be just fine." She suggested I try another form of birth control after the Depo Provera had depleted out of my body in nine weeks. I declined and discussed planning to use condoms for protection. I did not want to experience any further symptoms of any other contraceptive.

At the end of the semester, I failed three of my four classes. I tried pleading with my professors to allow me to complete extra credit. However, one by one, they told me I should have withdrawn from the class or written a letter to my Dean. I was even more depressed. I had no one to talk to. I had stopped going to church months ago, and I was too ashamed to go back. One of the Ministers from my church reached out to me, but I was too embarrassed to call him back. I could not talk to my mother about how I was feeling because she was still mad at me for leaving her house to stay with Josiah. My mother wanted me to make better decisions because my vision was clouded in her opinion. Here I was hanging on by a thread. All I could do was pray. I asked God to help me and keep my mind. My life had become depressed, overwhelmed, and full of uncertainty. It was now just God and me. I had to deal with me with no distractions. I had to deal with who I had allowed myself to become. I had been chasing after unrealistic relationships which I had created in my mind. I was wasting time, settling for people who God did not create for me. For so long, I had drowned out God's voice. He would whisper to me, "Leave that one alone, stop talking to that one, cut the conversation short with that one, run from that one, that one is going to hurt you, change your phone number." However, I followed my own thinking and feelings for men; through this I unknowingly created soul ties. God gave me free will. His scripture says I had to choose life or death. Now feeling depressed and out of my mind, I realized I had chosen death. This was a process I had to endure, which sometimes caused me to hang my head down in shame. Back in the mirror I went, speaking life over myself using God's word to bring myself back to life. After several weeks, I began going back to church. I went back to the choir stand, and I stood tall and strong as I came back from the fight of my life.

During my last semester of school, my mother called me to ask if I could keep Michael. Lehigh had gone to Michael's school and whooped Michael for acting up in class. Michael was in the sixth grade, and I was not sure why Lehigh thought it was okay to go to a middle school to reprimand him. My mother informed me Child Protective Services had come to her house and informed her about the investigation. The caseworker informed my mother that Michael had to go to another relative's residence until the investigation was completed. I quickly went to my mother's house to pick up Michael and his belongings and moved him into my one-bedroom apartment. My motherly duties had just begun. I took Michael to and from school and helped him with his homework. I made time to spend with him before he ate dinner, showered, and went to bed. I felt sad for Michael knowing that he was subject to Lehigh, knowing how controlling he was. If my mother was anything like she was with Brandy and me, Lehigh got his way when it came down to Michael. I attended class and came home to take care of Michael. Thank God I had experience from taking care of Aunt Rose's children. I knew exactly what to do. I applied for a two-bedroom apartment in another apartment development so that Michael could have his own bedroom. I got him a bed, and my father gave me a television for his room. However, after three weeks of Michael staying with me, CPS found there was no evidence to warrant a removal of Michael from my mother's residence. I called the CPS caseworker and discussed my concern for Michael returning to my mother's residence with Lehigh. This caused the investigation to continue, and my mother was not happy with me. I expressed my concern for Michael with my mother, who in turn, hung up the phone on me.

A week before Michael and I were to move into our new apartment, the CPS worker called me to inform me that she found no reason to keep Michael out of my mother's care. Despite Michael moving back home with my mother and Lehigh, I had to move into the new apartment due to signing the lease. I was not happy Michael had to move back with my mother and Lehigh. I was getting used to him living with me. We made it work, and we were both happy, enjoying each other's company. It was hard for me to focus on my last semester of school. I was constantly worrying about Michael after he went back to my mother's residence. All I could do was pray for him. I could not allow myself to fail another semester. Despite going through family issues, I had to keep pressing on and trusting God. I remembered Michael gave his life to God, and he was God's child. On my days off from work, I often visited Michael at my mother's house, trying to keep it cool with her and Lehigh so they would not stop me from visiting him.

Once the semester was over, I called my mother, my father, and other family members to invite them to my graduation. I was so excited that I was earning my Bachelor's degree. Despite all that I had gone through in college, I made it out. On the day of graduation, I did not see any of my family or any friends I had invited. Although I was extremely disappointed, I had to pull it together. This was my day, whether my family or friends were at my graduation to support me or not. I had endured and, with God's help, I had earned my degree. I remember the Dean of my Department calling each student's name as the crowd cheered for their loved ones who were graduating. Knowing no one was there to cheer for me, I soon started to cry, I bit the side of my jaw to prevent further tears from coming down my face as my emotions tried to overtake me. It was at that moment I heard the whispering calm voice of God in my ear, saying, "I am with you, and I am proud of you." As I sat in my chair, I remember sitting back and closing my eyes for a moment thinking, 'If nobody was happy for me or pleased with me, God was.' Despite all the foolish decisions I had made, God was still with me. That was better than anyone coming to my graduation.

Once my name was called, I walked across the stage to receive my degree. I was so excited. I had a smile on my face as if God was physically walking with me. I heard the crowd of people clapping and cheering like they all knew me. I received my degree with great confidence and with exceeding gratitude. I was very proud of myself because, once again, I made it through the raging storms. I had overcome every adversity that was thrown at me. Everything from my family hardships, to life's disappointments, to feeling like I was losing my mind. After my graduation, I drove home listening to Fred Hammond's "O Give Thanks". I was singing and crying at the same time for this scripture of song had become my testimony! I went home and praised God, dancing in the middle of my new living room floor. I thanked God and, before I knew it, I had begun crying and worshiping God. It was a worship that brought forth a breaking, and finally a release. It was my fresh wind.

TURNING POINT

"And we know that all things worked together for good to them that love God, to them who are the called according to his purpose."
Romans 8:28

───────────◈───────────

Six months later, I started working as a Day Treatment Counselor at an elementary school in the city. I had four first grade students on my caseload, two were brothers. All the students were African American. They were from single-parent households in high crime neighborhoods. The students all seemed to want two things; genuine love and attention. They all had anger issues that they would display if they weren't allowed to do something they wanted to do; if they did not know how to express themselves appropriately; or if they did not understand how to complete a task. My responsibility was to teach the students coping skills to express themselves in positive and appropriate ways.

I had one student on my caseload, Jonathan, who often became agitated when he did not want to complete his classwork assignments. He often had difficulty expressing himself appropriately. He would flip over his desk and run out of the classroom. He would also become disrespectful when interacting with me or his teacher, Mrs. Jones. The other three students; Larry, Nate, and Jerry, would argue amongst themselves and sometimes physically fight. Mrs. Jones and the other students in her class often watched to see how I would redirect their behavior. After countless redirecting, one on one sessions, and different behavior modifications we got through their rough patches. A bright smile would appear on their faces. I worked extremely hard and diligently with each one of the students. Some days I would just go home often feeling worn out after my workday.

Mr. Drake was another Counselor who worked in Mrs. Jones' classroom. He worked one to one with Timothy. Mr. Drake often shared with me the behavior modification strategies he utilized when working with Timothy. He always discussed how the public-school system needed better regulations for problematic students. Mr. Drake was highly intelligent. He knew his history and frequently shared his concerns about the world systems and his views on the past and present inequality systems in America. For some strange reason, the way Mr. Drake thought made me attracted to him. He had become my fantasy history teacher and I was his student. He stood at 6'5 and 220lbs with sandy brown dreads. His name-brand LRG pants always matched his LRG creative design shirts. He smelled like the potent scent of weed and scented oil. One day he brought me lunch as we talked about life outside of work. Mr. Drake and I exchanged phone numbers and had planned to hang out some evenings after work. It had been two years since Josiah, so I was glad to have someone to hang out with.

Within a few months, Mr. Drake and I started hanging out. I got a better understanding of who he was as he began telling me about his childhood. He explained how one of the students I worked with in Mrs. Jones' class reminded him of himself. He stated he was diagnosed with ADHD at a young age and had taken Adderall to help with his symptoms. He discussed having past issues with anger as if he still was unable to control his emotions. I thought in my mind, *'Please Lord, don't let Mr. Drake be another Mathis in disguise.'* I never shared much about my childhood with him, I just listened and offered advice that Mr. Drake could use while coping with his past. He once told me, "Yo, why do you talk to me like you are my therapist or something?" I thought to myself, *'Maybe because you need one.'* Instead of saying that, I just laughed and said, "I can be for a small fee."

Some Sundays after church, I would go straight to Mr. Drake's house to talk about the sermon preached by Pastor James. He never had much interest. He would always change the subject by asking me how I was doing or what my plans were for the week. He did not believe in Jesus Christ. He did, however, believe in God. We would have debates about God and different scriptures in the Bible. When I was unsure of the answer to his questions, I always invited him to my church. I made sure to estimate church as being one-hour longer just in case Pastor James was a little long-winded. However, he would always have something else to do or just declined.

One night, while hanging out at Mr. Drake's house, he made dinner for the two of us before inviting me to his in-house studio. He played around with different music beats as I would sing in his enclosed foam cased closet with the microphone hanging from his tall ceiling. I sang songs from TV shows or songs I made up and concluded my performance with a poem I had created for Mr. Drake. He played back the songs I sang as we laughed and made jokes about how I was off-key. We laughed throughout the night as if we did not have work in the morning. While in Mr. Drake's in-house studio, he went into his closet and pulled out a big black trash bag full of weed. He laughed at my expression as he began separating the bunches of weed to separate, roll, and smoke. He offered me some, but I remembered my promise to God at the age of thirteen, a promise that I clung to and planned to keep. With no hesitation, I quickly declined. It was at that moment I realized that this was Mr. Drake's way of coping with his past problems by smoking weed and drinking a glass or two of Hennessy. I addressed my concern with Mr. Drake of my observations, but he quickly replied, "I'm good baby girl. I used to be an alcoholic, but those days are over. I just casually drink, but I will always smoke my bud." You would have thought by now I would've gotten my things and went home. However, I stayed over anyway. We stayed up most of the night laughing and talking about the weirdest things despite having to work in a few hours. Our all night hang out sessions often lead to us spending the night at each other's apartment.

Although I was enjoying Mr. Drakes' attention, it was not long before I would receive a phone call from a woman who said she and Mr. Drake were in a committed relationship. She wanted to know why I had been calling him. It was at that moment I would get into my first phone confrontation with another woman about a man. I called Mr. Drake, asking him about the woman that called me. However, he insisted that they were no longer in a relationship. He discussed the breakdown of their relationship and the strain she had caused him. It was at that moment, I decided to believe him. I would see Mr. Drake at work, and I soon noticed my focus was more on him than the students with whom I worked. Mrs. Jones noticed it too. She had a conversation with me about her observation of Mr. Drake and me. She jokingly told me my nose was wide open and I must close it at work. Surprised at her response, I moved my work area and stopped interacting with Mr. Drake at work. I had gotten to a place where I came to work just to work. I started pulling back from Mr. Drake, who laughed at Mrs. Jones's response when I told him. I soon noticed Mr. Drake's behavior around other women while at work. I was starting to replay the conversation with the woman who called my phone saying she was Mr. Drake's girlfriend. I started to believe her. I thought, here we go again with the dysfunctional relationships. I was not going through this again.

Thankfully, Spring break was a few days away, I packed a bag and went to New Jersey to visit cousin Tameka. I had not seen her since Grandma's funeral. I told her my plans of moving out of Virginia and to New Jersey. I expressed my need to find employment and, surprisingly, Tameka put on her shoes to take me to several Human Services agencies where I applied for employment positions. While at the Youth Agency Center, I met Daniel. He worked at the center as a Residential Counselor. Daniel discussed his job position before giving me his phone number to call him if I needed anything. The following day, I left Tameka's house forgetting to give her back her house keys as she left for work. Once she arrived home from work Tameka and I began arguing about the keys because I accidentally locked her keys in her house. Tameka then called her friend Tangie, who soon met Tameka at her house to give her the spare key so she could get into her house. After I entered Tameka's house, I packed my clothes and went to Uncle Larry's house in West Philadelphia. Aunt Roxanne made my visit so welcoming. I did not know the area and I was a little bored. So, I called Daniel, who came to Uncle Larry's house and took me to South Street. There were so many people outside walking around the crowded streets that were full of beautiful faces. This was my first time on South Street. We stopped at a pizza shop and ate pizza while sharing pieces of our lives. Daniel was cool to hang out with. He was not loud when he spoke, nor did he use any profanity. He just smiled after each sentence. Just chill, like he was glad to be out.

The next night, Daniel came out to Uncle Larry's house late in the evening when he got off work. We sat on Uncle Larry's porch, talking, and laughing. However, after the third person had walked up to us while we were talking, asking us to buy items that may have been stolen or handmade, we decided to leave and drive around the city. While hanging out with Daniel, he told me he was in a relationship and had a daughter. The three of them lived together in New Jersey. Daniel discussed how his relationship was complicated and having a child made his relationship more complicated. Listening to Daniel speak made me think of how my life would have been if I had children. It also made me re-evaluate my relationship with Mr. Drake, who had called me several times during my trip. I believed I had better heed to this warning. Daniel did not know how much he was helping me through his conversation. Though I had been through enough, I guess this was my reminder. After returning to Uncle Larry's house, I looked over at Daniel and thanked him for his story. He smiled and said, "You're welcome." That night was my last time seeing Daniel.

Once inside Uncle's Larry house, Aunt Roxanne quickly opened the door to let me into the house. As I walked inside, she told me that ten minutes after I left with Daniel, someone had let off several shots on Uncle Larry's porch. I knew it was only God that kept our lives, causing Daniel and me to leave before the group of guys came. I could not sleep, still thinking about what Aunt Roxanne told me. So, once I saw a break of light from the sky, I gathered my clothes, hugged, and kissed Aunt Roxanne and Uncle Larry, then hopped on 95 South. On my drive back to Virginia, I had time to think of another plan. I called Tisha and told her I wanted to move to Brooklyn with her grandmother. She told me she would talk to her grandmother to see if I could stay with her until I found a job and a place to live.

I went to my mother's house two days after I returned home. I told her about my vacation. She laughed during the whole conversation as if she had heard another conversation. She laughed like she had life again. After laughing, she said, "Joi' I hope you are not planning on moving?" I just smiled, and jokingly said, "Ummm, maybe." Though I did not come out and tell her at the moment that I was moving, I knew the conversation would soon happen. I hung out with Michael, who walked around the house as if he owned it. He seemed happy and apparently was given more freedom. Michael was spending the night at his friend's house and hanging out more. My mother had even bought him a pool that she placed in the backyard. I looked around the house and noticed Lehigh was not around. I asked my mother, "Where is Lehigh?" She told me he had moved out. My mother told me Lehigh had been having an affair and found himself a new place to live. My mother had no idea what Lehigh was doing until she found a deposit receipt for the new house he planned to rent. It was at this moment I realized that, for so many years, my mother was bound to a man. It wasn't until he left her, that she was able to find her freedom. My mother invited me to her house to eat dinner several times throughout the week. Brandy came to visit her from time to time, and Michael was being the King he was destined to be. He spoke with confidence and smiled more, he walked around the house with a new posture, as if he owned it.

When I went back to work, I saw Mr. Drake, I spoke to him as normal. I had no time to be mad. I was about to leave Virginia and the school year was coming to an end. Tisha even called me to tell me that her grandmother said I could live with her until I found employment and a place to live. I agreed to pay her two hundred dollars a month.

For the next three months, I perfected my plan to move. I started saving more money. I stayed in contact with Aunt Roxanne, I told her I was moving to Brooklyn. Then, she told me about my cousin Nate, who lived in northern New Jersey and could take me to Brooklyn. She did not ask him, but she was confident he would take me. She said, "His grandmother is your grandfather's cousin, so he is your fifth cousin. He'll do it, just call him and ask." Though I did not know cousin Nate, I was standing on Aunt Roxanne's word.

After two days I called cousin Nate. I told him who I was and asked him if he could take me to Brooklyn. Cousin Nate gladly agreed. He told me he would take me to Brooklyn and offered me a place to leave my car at his house. I thought to myself, *'God, is this really You?'* I could tell this was going to be a smooth transition.

A month before leaving, I had given my church a notice of my relocation. I visited my students at their residence as I had still been in communication with their parents. I visited my family, my Godmother, and my friends to say my good-byes. Mr. Drake noticed that I was not the usual Joi', due to distancing from him. It wasn't long before I gladly told him I was moving next month. He agreed and said, "God is with you because some things about me ain't right. It's a good thing you are moving away." I could have hugged him one last time because, for once, he was honest. It would be years later when Mr. Drake informed me that he had a mental illness. I thanked God in my head for allowing me to dodge another bullet.

I picked up Brandy from my father's house so that I could meet with her, Michael, and my mother to discuss my move to Brooklyn. Brandy and Michael were already aware. It was my mother who did not know. Despite our efforts my mother and I still did not have a real mother and daughter relationship. I used this moment to talk to her about the pain I felt since I was a child. I discussed the effects of not having a healthy relationship with her and my father. I told her how I had been looking for love and conversations with men that were not healthy. I had summed up my life of dysfunction. The house was quiet, as a river of tears flowed down my face. I did not know I was harboring so much emotion and pain until this conversation. I spoke with so much conviction that Brandy had walked out of the room. My mother made excuses at first, stating, "Well, I did the best I could do..." before finally apologizing. She noted that she had experienced the same cycle with her mother and father and did not realize she had repeated it. I gave my mother a warm hug that she once gave me when I was a little girl before leaving her house.

I took Brandy back to our father's house to inform him that I was moving. He just looked at me and said, "Why the hell are you moving all the way up there by yourself? See there you go, you making them crazy-ass decisions again." Although I wanted to, I couldn't tell my father how I felt like I had done with my mother. He was like Mathis, going from zero to ten real quick. He probably would have torn up his house in the process before putting me out. This type of behavior was expected from my father. This was my father's persona my whole life. He had no filter, was full of rage and anger, and swore he knew everything. I did not say one word. I thought one day he would understand. Later that day,

153

my co-workers had a special dinner for me. Everyone asked the number one question, "So what are you going to do in Brooklyn?" I confidently answered, "I am going to be a supermodel." Although, truthfully, I could have been a dishwasher at a local diner for all I cared, I was leaving Virginia.

On August 8, 2005, I packed up all my clothes in boxes and placed them in my car. I gave away all my furniture, and what I could not bring with me I stored at my mother's house. I left Virginia thanking God for all that I have been through. I thanked him even more for where I was going. I was so excited about my future. I remembered all the experiences that I had been through and how I had overcome them all. The words that were said to destroy me, the relationships that were not good for me, the setups, and setbacks that I had experienced were only preparing me for where I was going. I knew, *"All things worked together for good to them that love God, to them who are the called according to his purpose."*

As I got on the highway, I yelled out of my window my mother's favorite words when we drove to New Jersey as a child, "95 North here I come."

www.ingramcontent.com/pod-product-compliance
Lightning Source LLC
Chambersburg PA
CBHW072149090426
42740CB00012B/2193